The Positive Child™

2/19/05

For Dreum:

Many Blessings for
the continuation of your
beautiful mission.

I'm Love

Ivonne Delagh

The Positive Child™

♦

Through the Language of Love

Self-empowered Children Through the Practice of Affirmations

Ivonne Delaflor

iUniverse, Inc.
New York Lincoln Shanghai

The Positive Child™
Through the Language of Love

iUniverse, Inc.

For information address:
iUniverse, Inc.
2021 Pine Lake Road, Suite 100
Lincoln, NE 68512
www.iuniverse.com

Editorial Services:
Rabia Tredeau
rabia4@earthlink.net

Book Design and Illustrations:
Foster & Foster, Inc
www.Fostercovers.com

The author of this book does not give medical or psychological advice. The main intention is to share inspirational guidance for spiritual parenting.

ISBN: 0-595-32051-1 (pbk)
ISBN: 0-595-66469-5 (cloth)

Printed in the United States of America

This book is dedicated to all children of planet Earth.
To Alhia & Christian...
Leonardo, Alex, Naomi and all precious beings who will spread the message of
The Positive Child™ around the world
with their pure and divine presence.
To Chick Moorman, for your strength, courage, spirit and
enlightening wisdom that is most needed for all parents of the world.
And to the Positive Child nature of all human beings:
May this book be a grain of sand
for the joyful evolution of the child within all of us.

And Jesus addressed his disciples:
For the Child of True Humanity exists within you.
Follow It!
Those who search for it will find it!

—*Karen L. King*
"The Gospel of Mary Magdala"

Contents

ACKNOWLEDGMENTS

o o o o o o o o o o o o o o o o o o o o o o o o o o o o o o o o o o

The only real duty that parents have towards their children
is to assist them to awaken from their Maya
and realize God within themselves.

—The Bhagavad-Gita

I am grateful for the positive attitude toward life that my father always showed to me. I am grateful for the constancy of my mother in continuing her job and duties, no matter how difficult times could be. Both my parents have always showed me they are beautiful children of light themselves. I am grateful for the smile of my grandmother and her magical ways that always surprised me with hidden secrets. I am grateful to be alive, to be able to share the Positive Child with all of you and humbly offer it to the divine within all of us. I am grateful for the existence of the Positive Realm for all humans to be able to choose it whenever they wish. I am grateful for the consistency, patience and professionalism of my editor, Rabia Tredeau and the iuniverse team. I am grateful for the existence of Mr. Chick Moorman and Dr. Thomas Haller who are creating a huge impact on the world through the empowerment of children and through their wonderful book called *The 10 Commitments Parenting with Purpose*. I am grateful to my husband Enrique, whose support, in many different and special ways, made possible the creation of this book.

I also want to express my appreciation to all the volunteers that work at the Mastery Life non-profit organization: Rebeca, Cristina, Leticia, Francisco, Malena, Carla, Ulda, Abril, Paty and Cynthia…for they have not only demonstrated great service to the children of the world but also serve me as powerful mirrors and reminders of who I am and who I choose to be. To my friend Elsa, for her courage and dedication to the children of the world. And to Patricia Seoane for her extraordinary work with the children of LA CASITA.

Finally, I am grateful to you all.
May you spread your positive child nature wherever you go.

And from my heart to yours: Thank you...

THE POSITIVE CHILD
PRAYER

May I never forget who I am.
May I always choose Positive Thinking.
May I always choose kindness and love
As the experience of my life.

May I never forget how to play with gentleness and respect.
May I treat my body as the temple of my heart and soul.
May I smile and laugh with grand celebration in my life.

May I learn from my mistakes and tears.
May I see the positive in every situation in my life.
May I always celebrate my existence as a human being.

May I awaken into the realm of the child of True Humanity.
May I remind myself when I grow up
That I am a Positive Child forever!

FOREWORD

I have seen Ivonne Delaflor in action in a variety of situations over the past five years. I have watched her in relationship with her own children, with the children of the La Casita Orphanage, and with my grandchildren. I have observed her in front of workshop participants, as a workshop participant, and as an organizer of workshops and seminars. I have seen her with friends, relatives, acquaintances, and employees. I have also experienced how she interacts with me.

I tell you this so you will realize the implications of the following statement: Ivonne Delaflor teaches what she lives and lives what she teaches. She lives love. She talks love. She *is* love. Therefore, it does not surprise me that Ivonne suggested creating the book *The Positive Child Through the Language of Love.*

The old model of how to be an effective parent is based on coercion and control. Its attributes are shame, fear, and the threat of punishment. It focuses on obedience and compliance, while addressing the needs of adults rather that the needs of children. The old model would have us dwell primarily on teaching our children content. It would have us focus on motivating them to recite the alphabet, learning how to read and how to do subtraction problems. We would instruct them as to how to tie their shoes, play the piano, and hit a baseball. We would expect them to know the rules—all the rules—and follow them without thinking.

The Positive Child suggests a wider mission for our role as parents. It offers us an opportunity to look at our children and our influence in their lives in new ways—through the eyes of love. Ivonne suggests we perceive our parenting job as that of helping children become positive human beings. She offers us ways we can help them grow in spirit through the application of unconditional love that is consistent and intentional.

The Positive Child is a major shift in perspective on raising a healthy child. It speaks about raising a positive child but also changes the consciousness of the parents as they read and implement the strategies.

There is no other book that wraps raising children in the framework of the positive theme. This book talks about such notions as bliss, love, sacred space, boundless power, human feelings, choosing our thoughts, endless possibilities, the teacher within, peace, quiet time and many others. There is no other book that addresses these issues and does so in a way that parents can begin to value these concepts for their children.

Exploring how to help children learn positive thinking, how to trust themselves, and how to understand and express their true emotions are all areas spelled out in this remarkable book. Teaching children about the attributes of beauty, change, gratitude, oneness, miracles, enough-ness, and enjoyment also become central to this purpose.

While many parenting books on the market today are concerned with making kids mind, getting them to show respect, doing what they are told, *The Positive Child* teaches children and parents that they are powerful with unlimited potential.

The Positive Child is a work of love about love, concerning love and is being sent out timely into a fear based world.

Parents have not thought of the issues this book addresses. It is not a major part of the world dialogue which makes *The Positive Child* a very unique book.

In essence the Positive Child asks parents to BE love to teach love, to create love in their children. *The Positive Child* has faith in love while other books have faith in fear.

When you hear the word "graceful," what image comes to your mind? Do you think of a ballerina, an ice skater or a swan, perhaps? Yes, those things are graceful, and so is *The Positive Child*. It is grace-full, packed full of ways to put grace to use in your parenting.

This book demonstrates how to hold a child in a state of grace as you teach lessons, offer positive discipline, and model effective communication. It explains how to hold yourself in a state of grace as you parent, make mistakes, and learn lessons. Read on and become increasingly grace-full, speaking the Language of Love.

Chick Moorman
July 2004
Author of Parent *Talk, Spirit Whisperers, Talk Sense to Yourself* and co-author of *Couple Talk* and *The 10 Commitments, Parenting with Purpose.*
www.chickmoorman.com

INTRODUCTION

o o o o o o o o o o o o o o o o o o o o o o o o o o o o o o o o o

A man is literally what he thinks, his character being the complete sum of all his thoughts. As the plant springs from, and could not be without, the seed, so every act of a man springs from the hidden seeds of thought, and could not have appeared without them. This applies equally to those acts called "spontaneous" and "unpremeditated" as to those which are deliberately executed. Act is the blossom of thought, and joy and suffering are its fruits; thus does a man garner in the sweet and bitter fruitage of his own husbandry.

—James Allen, As A Man Thinketh

Welcome to the universe of the Positive Child. I welcome you with an open heart and with the hope that all children on the planet can experience a glorious life based on love, health and Positive Thinking. I have created this book for those courageous parents who are willing to learn to break through their own limitations and who are willing to love their children more and to respect their individuality and their miraculous lives.

This book is my little grain of sand. My heart is in this grain…for as a parent and a child myself, I have a deep longing for peace and laughter in our world. Children are so terribly abused and so little respected. I don't want to go into more detail about what is happening regarding children since you already experience the consciousness of it. Few are the parents and teachers who listen to their children or who are grateful for the time in the here and now to be with these precious divine beings.

Mental education and material greed have occupied, in a superficial way, the sacred space for love. Education is good for the mind…material things are part of this planet as well…but please…are these the main priorities in our lives? I believe and feel with all my heart that in order to have a balanced life, the number one priority (spoken by all sages and all teachers throughout the history of our planet) is first and…above all…LOVE.

The Positive Child through the Language of Love offers simple and practical wisdom for parents. When the ideas are implemented, they assist both parent and child to co-create a positive lifestyle environment nurtured through mutual respect of emotional, social and psychological growth. Self-empowered to choose the most positive aspects of life based within their innermost core of being where the child embraces all dimensions—spiritual, emotional and mental as one. A whole human being who is capable of manifesting a successful and blissful life.

Bliss is a state of fulfillment and joy that comes from within and a sense of benediction that arises from the openness of one's heart. Successful people are those who can see the opportunity that lies behind every situation—either a positive or a challenging one. Success is for those who can live their life in joy, with grand respect for themselves and others. It is feeling that gratitude of being and striving to do the best in life: work, school, relationships. A successful mind nurtures positive and healthy thoughts.

A positive attitude automatically sets positive goals, which deliver positive ways to achieve those goals in successful and respectful ways. The Positive Child manifestations can be applied not only in child raising, but in "parent raising," and in all endeavors we perform. The positive outcomes we desire increase the percentage to manifest them. It is said that the best golf player first visualizes where they want the ball to land. Preparing the mind and energy manifests a goal and achieves the desired result.

The Positive Child lives life in *the moment*, makes the most of today, while building a firm foundation for the choices he creates as he grows. Honest and truthful opportunities will create a life which is abundant in possibilities and a life full of Love. This book serves as an easy, simple and effective tool for parents who are concerned about the spiritual aspect of their child's life. It may open a parent's eyes to see that parenting is a joy of love. The question then becomes *how does a parent guide their child when the world is in such a state of fear and anxiety?* There is a constructive, honoring way to respond to anxiety in our lives, whether as an adult or as a child. We must first trust ourselves and our children to be confident. We then can love them with a grand passion, determination and respect for their individuality. Pointing out the positive in life, praying for the good in everything, practicing and demonstrating love together delivers subtle tools for all to live a life of love, for it is said that it is LOVE that will lead us to greater peace. As parents, we know that in all things love works for the good of those with whom we share it.

This book is a portal for the parent who is willing to share laughter and life, true celebration, to embrace tears of joy with their children. It is for those parents who are willing to admit their mistakes. It is for anyone who is courageous enough to acknowledge children as human beings and who is willing to listen to the natural wisdom of all children. It is for all of us who embrace the possibility of growing more in *love* for a balanced evolution of their child's soul.

In order to assist children to empower themselves as a Positive Child, we must first become a Positive Parent and awaken into the awareness of our positive human nature. Read this book if you are willing to affirm unto yourself:

I am a Positive Parent
I am a Positive Human Being.

It is well known and scientifically proven that the people who practice Positive Thinking and have a positive attitude are the ones who smile more, share more, give more, and believe more in the positive things in life.[1] Therefore, they manifest abundance in all realms of reality. That is also true in my experience. I've seen miracles happen just with a positive thought. Faith, love and kindness are qualities of the Positive Beings…and these qualities have tremendous power to create miracles…to create more love.

The Positive Child is needed on our planet more than ever.

Don't you want your child to be blissful?
Don't you want your child to be loved?
Don't you want your child to succeed in all the projects he or she takes on in their life?
Don't you want to be a Positive Child yourself?

Well…if you want these things, say, *"Yes!"*…Say it aloud…Say it proud!
Say to yourself, "I want my children to embrace life with joy, freedom, courage and strength…to be kind, respectful and responsible. I want my children to

---

1. A study in the August 2002 issue of *Mayo Clinic Proceedings* reports that people who expect misfortune and who only see the darker side of life don't live as long as those with a more optimistic view. In addition, researchers also found other health benefits related to positive attitude. In the study, optimists reported fewer problems with work or other daily activities because of physical or emotional health; increased energy. They feel more peaceful, happier and calmer, have less pain and experience other positive health benefits. (See http://www.cnn.com/HEALTH/library/MC, and http://sln.suny.edu/courses/2004.)

be happy and free! I want my children to be positive children through the Power of Affirmations and the Language of Love."

If you've read this far, this is your call to become more loving, more peaceful, more open, more you. The time has come for the power of love to heal, for the power of growth to speak and for the Positive Child to love and play in this magical world. You can serve as a light for these precious human beings called "children." This can be your creation, fueled by the love for your children, your love for existence, and the love for yourself.

I believe that we, as parents, can co-create a way to remind children who they are. Remember that children are naturally positive, loving, joyful, free beings, and they can choose to create these qualities in themselves consciously, in a positive, affirmative way. The Positive Child has a positive sense of himself or herself. They feel that they have something important and worthwhile to share and contribute to the rest of the world. The Positive Child embraces challenges while celebrating and respecting life. They are confident beings, able to venture out into the world.

How many of us were told when we were little, "You have a choice. Your power within you is boundless. You create your reality. You can always choose love"? I think we heard this very rarely, if ever. Only a few people I know were ever supported and loved that way.

Imagine the possibilities if you serve as a channel of love and guidance for your children. Just imagine the possibilities of their creation as positive human beings. The time has come to let children know of their power and the potential of their choices. It is the right moment to let children in on this "secret" truth. While many institutions, schools, religions and techniques are focused on the mental abilities of a child, I know there is even more than that—something more subtle, so mysterious that it carries the essence of life, of creation, evolution and Source. That is the essence of the Positive Child.

Parents, teachers and caretakers are crucial in the demonstration of the positive experience of life for children. I believe this book could assist anyone responsible for the care of a child, to guide them with love, truth, freedom, simplicity and Positive Thinking while empowering and nourishing that child's spirit. A Positive Child can be encouraged to create himself as a being with positive thoughts, in a positive environment and with positive emotions, embraced by the power of love, kindness, spirituality and truth.

The Positive Child is a human being of power, intelligence and love, and the master of his own thoughts, holding the key to every situation. The Positive Child contains within himself the tools with which he may create himself as he wills, fashioning his thoughts to fruitful manifestations. The Positive Child is aware of cause and effect and embraces patience and practice as his allies. The Positive Child chooses to believe himself or herself to be a loving, positive and successful human being.

The Positive Parent embraces and lives the qualities of the Positive Child within his or her own being, choosing to teach through the living demonstration of the positive aspects of life. The Positive Parent sets healthy limits and firm roots through the *Language of Love*. The journey of being human is, in truth, a journey of love.

May this book assist you in cultivating your power within, accessing the love that you are, and connecting to your inner child always. May children never forget who they are. Receive my gratitude and "Source-full" embrace. Enjoy the journey—a journey of love-filled possibilities—and welcome to the universe of *The Positive Child*.

As a man thinketh in his heart, so is he...

PART I
THE WAY FOR THE
POSITIVE CHILD

o o o o o o o o o o o o o o o o o o o o o o o o o o o o o o o o

It is only with the Heart

That one can see rightly.

What is essential is invisible to the eye.

—Antoine de Saint-Exupéry

PART I
THE WAY FOR THE POSITIVE CHILD

1. THE PATH OF LIGHT

We all are One, despite our physical differences, the language we use, or the environment we live in. There is no *smarter, better, worse, dumber, wrong or right*. Oneness is the freedom from such concepts and comparisons. No matter how much we are told to do or feel in a certain way, we never stop being this *Oneness*, and we always have a choice as to how we want our lives to be. We "all-ways" have a choice, and with our decisions, we can create more love inside us and decide to create more positive experiences, manifesting through the choices that allow us to see who we really are…as love, as Source, as *One Consciousness* recreating itself constantly.

Life is simple and the path we choose to journey on should be endured as simply as possible. Creating a positive mind in children and in ourselves through *Positive Thinking* allows us to create simple thoughts and experience less complexity and misunderstanding in our lives. Then the essential simplicity transforms into an easily palpable reality.

We all are "power-full" beings with a grand capacity to love. With this capacity we can journey through our lives with light and delight. We are the embodiment of life and freedom. Our choices are unique, and each is valuable and honored. The awareness is that you are creating a choice; you choose the path you want to live your life on and the path you want to offer to your children. With this awareness, choose to remain open in your heart while you walk through the Path of Life. Allow your children to see this openness of yours. Remember, you can choose; you know the way in your hearts, for *You are the path of Love, The path of Light.*

2. THE LANGUAGE OF LOVE

There is only one way of communication that I recognize as being globally understood, and it is the Language of Love. When tears are shed by children on the planet, no matter what their race or religion, everyone understands. Everywhere in the world, a smile is recognized, as well. Through a hug, anyone can relate to the expression of closeness and love. A hug needs no words; you do not have to go and say, "Hey, I am hugging you!" You just hold someone and transmit your love through the embrace of it.

Laughter—I hear it in all countries, no matter how different the ideals are. A kiss is a kiss, wherever I go. A caress: the look of a mother to her newborn. The laughing eyes of a child are wonders to behold—the celebration of children for being alive.

Imagination…
Silence…

Through the Language of Love our requests to our children are based on our positive language, an important tool that creates a safer and happier environment (in both thoughts and emotions) for our children and for us. The best part of the Language of Love is that *all humans know it*! You don't need to go to language school to learn it. It is your birthright! We have to study French or Italian, but we don't need translators to understand this language; our hearts knows it so well. We know it because *we are love*, and what we are speaks stronger than mere words, conditionings, behaviors, or life situations. The love that we are and the love that we came here to be *is* the Language of Love.

Children of all ages speak this language all the time—when a toddler falls and cries and wants his mommy to hug him, when a newborn is held for the first time by his dad, when a child starts to walk, when he starts to talk, when she learns to eat, when he becomes more and more independent each day. In the meantime, you watch—and without words the love you send manifests itself through teaching, caring, nurturing, disciplining, feeding, holding, assisting—all the ways love is expressed.

Having had the opportunity to serve as a meditation teacher for children, but mostly as a mother of two little gurus, I've seen the most amazing transformations happen in children, even when their parents considered them a "problem" or thought that something was really wrong with them. Children in the class who were allowed to just be themselves—to learn the name of their emotions, to play, sing and listen to affirmations (which I constantly use during the class)—were transformed into more peaceful children *without ceasing to be children!* They were invited to be the children they already were!

It is true that we all know the Language of Love. It is true that we all are love, but it is true as well that many people live in fear. This fear creates a choice not to use the Language of Love.

There are endless studies about how important nurturing and touch are for the healthy development of children. Even the American Academy of Pediatrics has recognized the following as the most important factors in the development of children: enjoying your child, communicating in an honest and open way, and (most importantly) demonstrating your love to your child!

We know the language. I know and can assure each of you that even the most fearful beings, the coldest minds, have the longing for love inside their heart.

What I say to you is *open up.* Hug your child. Tell him how much you love him. Celebrate her tears. Delight in her laughter. Learn from his play. In silence, watch the evolution of the flower that they are, and in the process, smell the fragrance of your own evolution, your connection with the Divine, the love that you are.

Imagine or pretend that fear does not exist inside you anymore. Feel safe and be assured that sharing love, being love, expressing love cannot hurt or damage you. Love is, above all, the gift to oneself. Love yourself; share yourself with your children.

Your children are constantly learning from you. It has been said that the pupil always surpasses the teacher. Be aware that this can also apply in the negative expressions of life. What do you want your children to learn from you? Do you truly think that they only learn what you verbally teach them? Of course not! They learn from what they hear and from what they don't hear. Children respond to both your spoken and unspoken messages. They feel—and remember this always—they are as open as the sky. That is why many people say children are like sponges. Be aware of what you are doing, as well as what you are saying!

Who do you want to be? What type of teacher are you? What do you want to teach?

Neurons in the brain connect when positive events happen and they disconnect with negative events. How do you envision your child's mind and your teenager's mind? What are you willing to contribute, through the Language of Love, to make sure that their brain works in a balanced way?

Share love, give love, be love!
Hug your child, kiss their feet, and caress their hair—always from a space of deep respect for their bodies and their individuality.

> "I hug you" is the same as I love you.
> "I kiss you" means I love you.
> "I laugh with you" equals I love you.
> "I cry with you" means I love you.

Children all over this planet can understand and identify the feelings of sadness in a tear, comfort in a hug, the sound of laughter. Mozart is Mozart all over the planet; his music needs no translation. The same is true for love. The fragrance of a rose is the same all over the world. The only thing needed is for you to choose to be it, to express it and to create it.

For those of you who prefer a more left-brain explanation, contemplate this: "Giving love means more than just saying 'I love you.' Your child can't understand what the words mean unless you also treat him with love. Be spontaneous, relaxed and affectionate with her. Give him plenty of physical contact through hugging, kissing, rocking and playing. Take the time to talk, sing, and read with her everyday. Listen and watch as she responds to you. By paying attention and freely showing your affection you make him feel special and secure and lay a firm foundation for his self-esteem."

Some of the parents in my meditation classes thought this quote was from a meditator or mystic. To their surprise, it is actually from the *Complete and Authoritative Guide: Caring for Your Baby and Young Child* by the American Academy of Pediatrics.

Have you ever heard the song "All You Need is Love"? Well, I use the title of that song as a strong belief in my life and try to transmit this to my children as well. Love is essential, and so are food, water, clothes and shelter. When you are loved and love someone in return, the sense of power within is grand. It is an experience like no other.

Love your child unconditionally. Don't try to fix something that is not broken or try to change your child into another person. Your child is unique and she/he is a gift from existence to you. They are the most pure reflection of who you are. Speak the *Language of Love* to them and you will have given your child and yourself as a parent a great start.

Remember that you are not meant to be with your children forever. Beware of the words "If only I said…" or "If only I did…" *Say it now: love. Love now.* There is no other moment. Your child is waiting. Affirm to yourself all day long, every minute of your existence, *I am love*—and share this with your children in your own unique ways.

Love heals. Believe in it. Become it. Choose it. Create it. Be it.

What is the Language of Love? Is it a language that includes kindness, firmness, respect, joy, willingness to listen, to withdraw, to accept and guide without wanting to own our children whatsoever? It is all of these things, and it includes the power of unconditional love. If you want to know more about this, go *now* and look into the eyes of your children. They are speaking to you with the Language of Love, saying, "I love you, as myself—*I am love!*"

Your child is waiting for you to respond. What are you waiting for?

3. POSITIVE AND NEGATIVE

Every parent that I know—well, at least almost all of them—wants their son or daughter to be a Positive Child. They want to have a child who has been empowered. They want someone who is responsible, capable, and respectful. They want someone who knows how to overcome the problems that manifest themselves in their lives with strength and an optimistic attitude. Yet, what tools are you giving to your child to truly make this a possibility? What are you providing for them to pursue positive choices as a constant in their lives?

I often hear parents say to their children, "No! That is wrong!"

"Don't do that!"

"You did it again!"

"You don't behave well!"

"Good children don't do what you did!"

This choice of language, from my experience, is a language that lacks teaching, explanations, love, true communication and *positive empowerment* for children! If you truly want to assist both you and your children to become a Positive Child, then you must begin to bring consciousness to the feelings, thoughts, and emotions that you communicate with your children and with yourself!

Having an intention and awareness on the positive impact (or vice-versa), we can model empowerment for our children with our actions, feelings and thoughts to diminish power struggles and resentment. We, as Positive Parents, need to provide the healthy limits and the positive guidance that our children need.

Promoting positive ways to see and experience life enables our children to increase their self-esteem. This can be done through honest, descriptive praise, recognizing with the heart the positive attitudes and actions that our children are creating.

Regarding the raising of their children, I've heard many parents say: This is the way I was taught."

"This is the way it works for me."

"This is the way our grandmother did it, and if it works, why change it?"

"This is the way my children obey me."

"This is how I let my children know who is in charge!"

"Sometimes hitting children is necessary, because they are only children!"

Well, for me, all these opinions and clichés are wonderful ways to delude us into thinking that we are being loving and responsible with what we say, think and do with our beloved children. Words are amazing tools to remind us not to be lazy in remembering that on the journey of parenting one must not stop learning, researching and becoming a better human being every moment of one's existence. On this journey we must be willing to listen to advice, to request assistance, even ask for help in order to be more loving, more balanced and more respectful.

If you believe that hitting, violence and harsh words are the tools that will help your children become better human beings, then this book is not for you! Yet I welcome you with all my heart to read it anyway. It might assist your child within. In the process your positive child nature may emerge while the reading occurs and might assist you to remember that what you wanted and needed most as a child was above all love, only love. That is the first step.

I'm going to ask you this—right here, right now. Do you really want your children to be positive kids? Do you truly want them to be and feel free? Do you want them to feel great about themselves and love being human beings?

First, we must understand that in order to choose the "positive," we must first recognize what is "negative." We must begin with ourselves. We cannot say to our children, "You are a Positive Child" when in our minds we have negative thoughts or think that the positive simply doesn't exist. We must teach by demonstrated actions. If we want our children to be respectful, we must show respect first. If we want them to practice silence, we must practice silence ourselves! This requires consistency, focus, and a willingness to admit mistakes, learn in the process, and then continue with this wonderful opportunity of parenting.

Parents constantly forget that their children need to learn about the negative, too. Parents will go on saying," Don't do that! That is bad!" "That is wrong!" and so on *without explaining,* thinking that this is the positive way to educate or guide children. We as parents often look for the perfect behavior, the model child that will grow to have the finest manners, the best grades at school, the proper clothes, even be spiritually perfect! With so many "expectations" for your child to be "perfect," where does love, uniqueness and free choice fit? Where does a positive child—one who knows freedom, trust and love—enter the picture?

What is it that is bad? Is it bad to cry? Is it bad to have tantrums when you are three years old? Is it positive to hit your child to educate him? To call him names or threaten her? To tell him how things have not been done the way you like them to be done? What about negative feelings or emotions? Don't you have these emotions yourself?

You must explain to your child what is bad, negative or wrong in order to offer them the tools to choose the positive in life. You must be very clear in your mind and heart what is really Positive Thinking and what is not. The best way to work with your children, and with yourself, to become more positive is through exercising repetition! Yes, you can train the mind through the wonderful power of *affirmations.*

Whenever your child is in what you call a "negative" state of being, please give them space to cool down. Allow yourself time to observe what is really happening. Is it negative, or is it just coming from your negative way of thinking or seeing things through judgments and habitual thoughts? When the waves are calmer, you can approach your child with love and firmness and comment gently about the behavior, emotion or action you just witnessed in your child's experience.

Remember that the positive and the negative are both part of the human experience. You just need to be acutely aware of what is positive, what is negative, and have a very clear intention to transmit this information to your child. You must also be willing to recognize the self-sabotage that you engage in with yourself and probably model for your children. You must be willing to experience trust—yes, *trust.* I believe that all is perfect in creation, and behind every event, the hand of God, the hand of Source is working to allow miracles to happen.

Let your children know that being positive and being negative is a choice. Assist them through repeating affirmations with them as your Language of Love. Explain constantly what is negative and acknowledge them when they are positive. Of course, since we are focusing more on the positive, continue to reinforce the positive thoughts and emotions they have and gently let them know when they are choosing the opposite (the negative) without giving too much power to that!

Focus on the positive. Acknowledge the negative as a tool to remind you that the choice of being positive is always available to you at any moment, in whatever situation. You just need to choose!

4. THE POWER OF AFFIRMATIONS

Just as a child can learn a complicated song by the mere repetition of it, positive phrases will get inside children's consciousness and offer them options and possibilities to create more power within, more joy and more love in their lives as they grow.

Mr. Chick Moorman says in his book *Talk Sense to Yourself,*

> "There are several theories as to why affirmations work. The religious theory holds that affirmations are like prayer. God hears the prayer (affirmation) and responds. A psychologist might suggest that affirmations are related to the subconscious mind. In that theory it is believed that affirmations plant ideas in the subconscious mind and when this part of your mind senses an appropriate situation, it sends your conscious mind a signal. You then act in accordance with what you have been affirming. A third theory is that thoughts have energy. The energy from an affirmation goes out into the world, has an impact on people and objects, and attracts situations and circumstances that contain similar energy patterns."

From my experience with myself and with all the people I have a close relationship to, I know that affirmations *work!* Affirmations are powerful prayers. They plant ideas in the subconscious mind that then make us act in accordance with the affirmation. As proven by scientists all over the world, thoughts carry energy and affirmations are energy!

Considering these three statements of Mr. Moorman's as facts, we must bring our whole focus and intention to creating Positive Affirmations and we must be very selective as to what we want to create through them!

I know many of you will say that affirmations are positive already, but that is not always the case. What about when people affirm to themselves, "I can't, I can't, I can't!" or "I hate you, I hate you, I hate you!"?

In *The Dhammapada,* there is a quote that I personally love to use as a reminder when I create "not so positive" situations in my life:

> You are what you think you are.
> All that we are arises with our thoughts.
> With our thoughts, we create the world.

What you think is what you get. Whatever you affirm unto yourself is most likely to manifest itself as reality in your life. The power of affirmations is grand—through singing, through writing, through prayers. The more you repeat something, the more you learn it and the more you believe that you *are* it!

Repeat many times to your children:

> *I am love.*
> *I am loving.*
> *I am loved.*

They will learn it. They will think it. They will repeat it. They will believe it. They will become it, and they will share this with the world. Therefore, we create more positive beings that create a more positive world for themselves and for the whole of humankind.

5. THE POWER OF CHOICE

A Positive Child must have the awareness that he has a choice. He has a choice to be happy or unhappy. She should know that she has a choice to wake up and say, "I choose to be happy today, to experience love, no matter what happens in my life," or to *not* say that.

It is important to let children know that choices exist. Many parents don't want to do that because they think they might lose control over their child. Please remember, however, that we are speaking about our beloved children—not some circus animal that we must train to behave properly in the show! Your children are human beings! They need to know they can choose to be happy in every moment.

Parents, are you aware that *you* always have a choice? Do you know that you can choose to be happy, choose to be loving? Are you aware that having more choice in your life increases your personal power? Events and people in our lives always put us in a position to make a choice.

The other day, my daughter went to a party. Two of the girls didn't want to play with her. I watched her face from where I was sitting and I could see that she was about to cry. I went over to her and whispered in her ear, "You either can choose to stay with these girls that have decided not to play with you, or you can choose to be with your other friends who are happily waiting for you over there." She gave it a thought, and then she made her choice. Of course she left the scene not-so-quietly, telling the girls a few things that I chose to ignore.

Whenever my children are in one of those endless tantrum episodes or are fighting with a sibling or friend, I just gently remind them, "Remember you have a choice." Then I ask, "Which do you want to choose—happy or upset?"[1] This is just an example of how I apply this Power of Choice with my own children. I have also found it to be very effective with older children, but that is a subject for another book!

I believe I have a choice to be happy. I believe that I can make a change. I believe that we all are capable of choosing, no matter what the situation or "problem" is in our life, to see the positive teaching in it.

---

1.   Researchers at Hope College in Holland, Michigan say forgiveness seems to be better for people than holding a grudge, at least in terms of the negative effects on the body. Lead researcher in the study, Charlotte van Oyen Witvliet, Ph.D. explains, "It may be that forgiveness holds its own type of healing." (See http://my.webmd. com/content/Article/21/1728_55258.htm reported by Mike Fillon.)

Many people say to me, "I have no choice; I am sad that this is happening." Unfortunately, I have little empathy for statements like, "It can't be!" or "I can't do it!" or "I'll never forgive them." I choose not to give a lot of power to decisions like that. I'd rather focus my intention and my attention on, "How can I make this happen?" or "I can do it with your assistance." It is most important for you to let your children know about this power of choice. Believe me, my friends; one day this power of choice, when we are not present with our child, will make a difference in their lives.

Consider when they are growing up and they begin to choose healthy food instead of junk food when you are not around. (Feels great, doesn't it?) What about when your children begin to choose to use their money wisely instead of just unconsciously spending it? If I venture into more important issues, such as when your teenager is offered drugs and with his power of choice he says, "*No!*"—Bingo!

A key, and a most important component here is the word *respect*. Through offering choices to our children and respecting their choices, we reinforce our child's self-worth, and our own, at the same time. I believe this can be done, but you must start with yourself—as a parent. You need to choose to be positive, to be happy, and to be alive in the moment.

You can choose to respect your children, to love them, to teach them, and to celebrate their uniqueness and individuality, or you can choose to pretend that you have no choices at all and watch the growth of your beloved children from a position of powerlessness.

Remind your children that *they have a choice*—a choice to be positive, a choice to be respectful, a choice to be love. Know, and let your children know of this: it is *your* choice.

6. MY EMOTIONS HAVE A NAME

It happens sometimes that you or your child will say things that are not really what you meant to say. Often these things might seem hurtful or without respect. The truth is that we need to learn to speak from the truth that we are and say things "just as they are." We must name our emotions in order to transcend them and transform them into clarity, mastery and love, "all-ways" from an open-heart state, and never compromising the truth.

Choose to say, "I feel angry" when you are angry and be fully responsible for it instead of projecting your anger unto others and trying to avoid the realization or reality that you are indeed angry. Choose to say, "I feel happy," when you are happy; "I feel upset," when things aren't going so well, and so on.

In my meditation classes for children and in my own house, I constantly (without being obsessive about it) offer a name for the emotions that my children are expressing. Why do I do that? Because if a child does not know what they are feeling, creating or thinking, how will they be able to choose a more positive emotion to feel?

Let me explain. Whenever my daughter tries to put her clothes on by herself and finds it difficult to put her shoes on or snap the buttons, she will scream, throw things, and say negative words. When I just go to her and say, "Baby, that is called frustration," she then has a name for what she is feeling and she can choose another emotion. Whenever a child feels jealous of their sibling, I just say, "That is called jealousy."

I try not to only focus on the negative emotions; I embrace the positive ones, too! I will say, "That is called sharing" when I see my son doing that or "That is compassion"—or devotion or kindness and so on when I see those qualities and emotions modeled.

To go one step further, in my meditation classes I say to the parents, "First explain the emotion you think your child might be feeling and then explain the opposite emotion. Tell your children, 'This is sadness; this is happiness.' Show them what love is, in relation to hate. I find it is easiest to explain these things to children through drawing."

Drawing is a helpful, practical way to clarify emotions and it gathers their attention, since you are speaking to children in their language. In Part IV: Practical Exercises for the Positive Child, I share the basic drawing exercise that I use in my "Meditation for Children" class. It is a down-to-earth fun exercise that you as a parent can do with as many emotions as you wish. You will find it may assist you as well in identifying emotions and making conscious choices.

7. BEING HUMAN

I am always surprised to see that the last thing we as parents teach our children is the simple fact that they are human. I mean, when do parents normally teach children this? When they are ten years old, perhaps? What I remember being taught at ten was anatomy—that a human being was a respiratory system, a digestive system, blood, cells, skin, organs, etc.

We live in a multi-cultural, multi-ethnical world, with a wide abundance of diversity! It's important for our Positive Child to know who they are. It is important for them to know and feel that they are valuable and needed for the world—that their contribution, just by being human, is a wonderful miracle of creation. That is what is valued and most honored.

It was not until I was in college and had attended an ethics class that I began to listen to and recognize world values. Human beings must have values: they must be good, they must respect rules, they should dress like this, eat like that pay taxes, and so on. This is information for the mind, which is fine, but to be a human being for me is far beyond flesh and bones. A human being is a temple, a miracle; it is the image of Love.

I invite all parents to share with your children the knowledge that your experience has given you—how magical it is to be a part of this wonderful world by being a human being. That is our way to experience joy, to celebrate life, to breathe the air, to watch sunsets, to listen to birds singing. It is truly a miracle!

Here is a message to welcome a newborn child into the world. I envision all people—nurses, mothers, fathers and doctors all over the world—using this blessing as soon as a child is born. Please remember, parents, that everything you say is stored in a child's subconscious forever, so please be mindful of your words. A simple message for the wonderful little minds of our brand new human beings could be, "Welcome to planet Earth. I honor you with love. You have a human body. You have a soul. You are pure energy. Being human includes emotions, sensations, feelings and thoughts. Welcome."

What better message to offer than the silent words of unconditional love? Can you imagine the birth of a child where everyone agrees to observe silence, at least for thirty seconds, as the child is born? What if we watch the bonding between child and mother while the only music, sound or words is perhaps the sounds of the new born baby and the beating of his heart?

This is just a model, just one example, for I believe that each parent could create their own personal blessing, full of their own truth and delight in the presence of their newborn being.

Don't you think that children at least need to know immediately after birth that they are living on a planet that is part of a huge universe? That in their experience of being human, they will have many wonderful opportunities to journey on a spiritual voyage disguised with many adventures? We all carry this information from within already—the grand awareness that we are. It comes from the natural knowledge, but we all serve as reminders to each other. Let the reminder be one of Love, Consciousness and Truth.

We must start with the simple facts to assist the newborn on the journey of discovering their God within and their destiny. Simple facts.... I know and trust that our Positive Children will find their way. They will meet their own power face-to-face, and they will make wonderful contributions to their families and to their planet as well.

Start with the basics. "Dear Child, you are a human being on a planet called Earth." Speak to them about their bodies. Let them know that they will grow. Speak about the facts—what they might be able to do since they have little legs, taste buds, tears—all the elements that embody our humanness.

This is so simple. I believe that after the words, "I honor you with love," the next words that you need to record in your child's mind are, "You are a human being!" I believe this is enough, for remember that beyond the words, the truth is transmitted, the love expressed, and the power of the Language of Love is felt.

8. MEDITATION

○ ○

"The Spiritual Guides the Mental. The mental guides the physical, not the other way around."

—*Swami Veda*

The art of going within is very ancient, and most needed these days with so much emphasis given to tragedy, to stress and to illness. It is time to be peaceful within. It is time to recognize that our strength does not reside in how much we do or how powerful our minds can be. Meditation is a time to tap into our internal power, into the love that we are—through silence, through respect and love.

We live on a noisy planet—even spiritually! There is too much information available, and we parents may be confused as to what is best for us and our children. We may not know what things should be studied or what should be done.

It is time we parents begin to meditate! To go within is to use the source of abundance in each of our souls so that we can move from this inner place and share the gift of peace, of real power—the Power of Love—with our children.

Let's do a practical exercise right now, you and me.

> In this moment I want you to slowly read this and be aware of your breathing…in this moment we are one…in this moment we are loved…in this moment we exist…in this moment, I love you.

Repeat these words if you choose to do so, and feel them with your heart.

Now remain in silence for one...

moment...

....

Breathe again.

This practical meditation exercise can be done at any time of the day, wherever you are, whoever you are with. You can create your own meditations for yourselves and for your children. I encourage you to do so.

There are wonderful teachers and schools devoted to encouraging meditation. Call it yoga, call it Reiki, call it mindfulness—whatever the name, the intention is the same.

Go within.

Breathe; be as present as you can be, in the here and now.

If you can transmit this to your children, you will teach with your experience, the importance of going within, of watching the mind and manifesting stillness. I believe, then, that your children will grow happier, their anxiety will decrease, their self-esteem will blossom and contentment in their life's journey will come naturally into their experience.

Some parents bring their children to my meditation classes and just leave them with me. I always invite both the parent and the child to stay for the class. I really would like to work with parents, because I find that children are in a naturally meditative, focused state, and they expand easily because they have less information or programming in their minds. Yet most parents never accept my invitation to stay and participate.

When the class is over, these children return to their homes and find it very loud and sometimes very tense. Parents often want their children to meditate, but they don't practice meditation themselves. There is no consistency for the child, and therefore an experience that could be very rich for both parents and children sometimes turns out to be more stressful for both of them.

With meditation, all beings start to vibrate on a subtle level and they become more settled, more balanced. As a result, they become more truthful, speaking the reality they see. Most parents don't like it when the truth their children are speaking doesn't fit with their programming.

I recommend to start with yourself. Begin to meditate; go within; create a minute of silence a day. Pray. Be grateful. All of this is meditation. Do your children a favor and treat yourself with grand compassion and respect. Go within, meditate; you deserve this time; you need to renew.

Yoga is also a powerful tool for focus, endurance and active meditation. For children, yoga is also great. It offers the practice of focus, quietness, stillness, concentration and coordination. It is a noncompetitive sport and increases self-esteem and awareness of breathing and life force.

Meditation is indeed a powerful tool to deliver balance, peace, and clarity to yourself and more space for you to choose love.

PART II
INSPIRATIONAL PRAYERS

o o o o o o o o o o o o o o o o o o o o o o o o o o o o o o o o o o
Truly, I say to you,
Whosoever does not receive the Kingdom of God
like a child, shall not enter it.

—*Luke 18:17*

21

PART II
INSPIRATIONAL PRAYERS

These inspirations are created for you, the Positive Parent, to read and share with your child. Read these prayers and explain to your child how they make you feel. My suggestion is to choose one each week to make sure that the ideas and positive affirmations are absorbed and understood by your child's precious mind. If your child can already read, so be it. Allow them to read the prayers to you. You can even suggest that they record a couple of them on tape so that with their own words they can listen and re-listen to these affirmational inspirations. You can also use them as prayers at night, before your Positive Child goes to sleep. Prayer is considered one of the most powerful meditations. It is a wonderful way to focus the mind and lift the spirit.

With these affirmations you will bond more with your child, creating special moments for both of you. In addition, most importantly, you'll be reinforcing not only the positive aspects of life in your child or children, but also in yourself.

As always, it is your choice...

1. BEING A POSITIVE CHILD

I always have a choice, and with my choices I can create more love inside me and a more positive experience of who I am in the way that I am. No matter how much I am told what to do or how to feel, I will never stop being positive as a way of life.

Life is simple. Positive Thinking is simple. I can choose to create my thoughts to be simple as well. Being the powerful, loving being that I am, I choose the choice-less choice of positive thoughts in the way of light.

I am the embodiment of life and freedom.

My choices are valuable and honored.

I am a Positive Child, a whole human being.

I am aware of my choices, and with this awareness I choose to remain open in my heart.

I can choose.

I am love.

I am positive.

2. JUST AS IT IS

I choose to say, "I feel angry" when I'm angry; "I feel sad" when I'm sad; "I feel happy" when happy; "I feel sleepy" when I'm sleepy; "I feel hungry" when hungry; and so much more. Why would I choose to say, "I'm angry" when I feel hungry, or when I'm sleepy, or when I feel sad?

I make the choice to say things just as they are—to speak precisely, in a descriptive, loving way. When practicing this, I train my mind to see things as they are. I choose to awaken my mind to the creation of no comparisons and judgments.

This is just as it is, and I am who I am forever—and even longer.

It's as simple as that.

This is it.

I am love. I am who I am.

3. I AM SPECIAL AND UNIQUE

All that I am is special, and others are special, too. We each have a particular job to do in this world that only we can do.

I naturally create what I want to experience when I choose not to compare myself with other people. I choose not listen to others regarding what they think I should do or how I should be.

I listen to my inner voice, which tells me that I am special. I know I am important for existence. I know that existence couldn't be as complete as I know it without other special beings, too.

By being unique, I make other people smile, and most importantly, that makes me smile.

I listen clearly to my heart and the stillness of my mind.

My special uniqueness spreads all around the Earth.

I share myself naturally and honor the sharing of others.

Everyone is special and unique.

So am I.

I am special and one-of-a-kind.

4. BEING LIKE A FLOWER

I am the seed and I am a flower that opens in many forms and multidimensional ways.

My possibilities as a flower are endless.
My fragrance comes from my open heart.
I like the smell of my petals.

How good it feels to be a rare and special flower!
There are many possibilities of coloring my petals.

In my life, I remember the flower, and always create possibilities of love, freedom and truth.

I enjoy watching my own evolution.
How colorful my petals are!
And you know what?
I smell really good.

I am a flower of Love.

5. I TRUST WITH MY EYES CLOSED

Sometimes the attitudes and things I choose are interpreted by others in a way I don't understand. Yet, whatever the interpretation is, I remind everyone around me to look at my heart.

With my eyes closed, I take their hands, put them on my heart, and their hands vanish.

With closed eyes, I trust my heart.

Others begin to trust their hearts too…

Now it is not just their hands that vanish, but their interpretations or judgments of certain attitudes or things.

It is good to know that even with my eyes closed, I can choose to be me.

Yes, me!

Peek-a-boo!
With my eyes open or with my eyes closed,
I am always who I am!

6. MOTHER WISDOM

My way is guided by a power
That is always creating itself as more.
It is the power of Mother Wisdom,
Who nurtures me with consciousness and love.

It's my eternal Mother,
The one who lives inside my heart
And manifests love with the choices I create.

Her lullaby is peace, stillness and bliss.
How much I like to listen to her song!
As I learn it, I can sing it to others, too.

Her love is endless,
My wisdom is, too.

I am wise.

7. MY TEACHER WITHIN

How wonderful it is that on this planet I'll learn many things.

How many beings will serve as the vessel for those many wonderful things that I will learn? Many teachers will guide me and enlighten the way I'm already choosing to walk.

Teachers are like magicians—they speak through all I know and give me the choice as to what I want to create. They always remind me of my teacher within.

My teacher within loves me unconditionally; the teachings are endless.

My teacher guides me to the place inside myself where he/she lives—constantly, through the power of kindness, respect and through the power of love.

My inner teacher reflects in the mirror of other beings. How fortunate I am to be guided by a teacher like this.

I choose to learn.

I choose to experience the positive teachings of my soul.

I am a student of love.

8. DIVINE OPPORTUNITY

I've seen that grown-ups around me sometimes forget who they are. I have an opportunity to choose the love that I am and the positive thoughts I create in my mind. While grown-ups sometimes create struggle to find their way back to balance, I watch and delightfully await balance by choosing simple activities that nourish my soul.

I choose a space that is clean and full of fresh air.
How much I enjoy the grass, my bare feet, the sound of my heart!
I remain serene and experience joy in the simple things of life.
I let grown-ups know that they also have a choice.
By smiling, I always do that.
Sometimes I don't need to even use words. Then they smile also.

I am a divine opportunity to be myself.
All-ways.

I am an opportunity.

I am divine.

9. CREATING MORE LOVE

I realize that the magic inside me creates more magic around me.
My habit is to create love, inside myself, in what I do.
When I play by myself or with others,
I always keep in mind my power to create more joy.

How wonderful it is to be a creator of reality!
How good it feels to be me!
I can be all that I want to be!

If you excuse me now, I have to go…inside myself to create more love.

Hey, what are you waiting for?
Hurry up!
Follow me!
Create more love, and more bliss.

I am creating love.

10. I AM PEACE

I choose peace.
I love myself being the way I am…

If I encounter situations of violence or negativity,
I remember that I am a powerful creator of peace.

I choose to start inside me,
For I know that my creation is of abundance,
Like a cascade of light, it spills from my heart.
I bathe in it always.

The peace I know is the peace of freedom.

I am peaceful.

I am peace.

11. GUIDING LIGHTS

The beings taking care of me are spirits of light that guide me on the way.
I choose to follow that which creates more love in my heart—for myself, for all.

How much joy I have,
Knowing that no one owns me or possesses me.
How much certainty there is in knowing that no one controls my destiny.
We all serve each other as guiding lights on the way.

My destiny is clear, it is my choice.

I am my own destiny.
I am my own destination.

I am the driver that will get me exactly where I want to go.
I am a guiding light.

Do you need a flashlight?

I am light.

12. MR. MISTAKE

I'll meet Mr. Mistake many times in my life. I am aware of his enormous power to teach me about life and possibilities. Sometimes he is disguised as things I say or things I do. He lets me know of the consequences of my actions. He is a great teacher. He points me on the road I should take in order to be happier and more loving inside.

How good that he exists, and how wonderful that he attends to every human being I know. I choose him as my friend.

I choose to learn.

Thank you, Mr. Mistake.

I am learning from you.

I am learning.

13. QUIET TIME

I am aware that I am stillness....
I have a special place inside me.

Whenever I choose to feel in a way that creates unpleasant sensations inside,
I immediately go to my special place.
As I enter, I recognize that it is the time for quiet,
For this place has wonderful, magical messages for me.

I am attentive to the messages that will guide me to feel better and choose to create things that will generate pleasant feelings.

Being still and quiet is good for my heart, mind and soul.
I love stillness; I am still.

In my quiet space, in my quiet time, I rest safely—happy and secure.

Shhhhhhhh...don't you see?

It is quiet time.

I am silence.

14. MAKING THINGS HAPPEN

Sometimes things happen just as I think of them.
Sometimes I work hard to experience what I want to create.

I know that I can make things happen.
I choose to think positively so that I generate positive things and experiences as the outcome of my creation.

I believe in making things happen.
I believe in myself.
I believe in what I create.
I am responsible for it.
I can make things happen, and so can you.

I am aware of my power...
I manifest positive things around me all the time.
I am making things happen.

What are you thinking now?

Are you making things happen?

I am me.

15. TRUSTING ONESELF

I look for validation in my own heart.
I trust myself and take care of this trust.
I fulfill myself with my choices.
It is not another person's job to fulfill me.
That is my job.

I trust deeply in my wisdom.

I am a powerful child, full of love and joy.
I trust this is the way to be.
It is my choice.

I trust others by first trusting myself.

I am trust.

Yes!

16. ENJOYING THINGS

I enjoy the things I have, see, create and experience. With detachment, I enjoy these things more. Sometimes some of us forget that things are toys that entertain us for a moment. When that happens, I remember that my happiness and enjoyment is coming from inside me—inside my heart, and not from the things I see or have. Then I easily remember again, and begin to choose to enjoy things without clinging to them.

Material things that I create are part of being human on this planet. I choose never to forget that these things are for my enjoyment. I choose to see them as the tools they are for sharing and entertainment.

I am aware that sharing is a good way to remind myself of this.

I enjoy things...

The thing I enjoy most—

Is being me!

I am enjoying myself.

17. MRS. CONFIDENCE

I know that whenever I feel nervous or in doubt, Mrs. Confidence appears, shining brightly to guide me. She must be an angel, for Mrs. Confidence is always with me. Wherever I go, whatever I do, and whatever the problem or challenge is for my growth, Mrs. Confidence speaks to me in her language of light and points me in the direction I need to go.

Mrs. Confidence loves me; that is why she chooses to live in my home, inside my heart.

Mrs. Confidence is very strong; she eats vitamins of love, praise, and bliss.

It's great that Mrs. Confidence is part of me.

We are one.

I am confident.

18. ENOUGH

I choose wisely the things I do, eat, play and say.

I know when to stop eating chocolate cake. I remind myself how much cake is just enough to take good care of my body.

I also know when there has been enough tears, enough screaming, enough silence, and enough thinking.

I choose to live my life; it's enough.

I love myself as I am; it's enough.

I like the way I laugh; it's enough.

I know when I have enough.

These are enough words for now.

I am enough.

19. QUALITY TIME

Sometimes some of us humans are in a rush because of time. Being a witness to this, I recognize the power of quality time.

When I am with others I love, I enjoy them dearly and choose not to waste a moment (when I'm with them, redundant) or choose not to make my words of love for them wait.

I create quality time to share with the ones I love.
I experience quality time with myself constantly.

By being totally present in the moment, fully enjoying who I am, I create more quality in my life through the experience of time.

I embrace the time I spend with others.

Whatever my experience, I choose wisely to create my time with love, quality and joy. Whenever someone speaks about quantity of time, I remember to smile inside and pursue the creation of more quality in it.

I choose with my heart to create quality time in the constancy of my experience as a human being.

I am grateful to have shared this moment of time with you.

I choose my time wisely

20. LOVE

Love is a wonderful sensation that I can create whenever I choose to do so.
Love is my essence.
Love is what I feel when I'm with the ones I like to be with.

I can choose to love my planet, the people around me, the animals and all that exists. Love is a choice, and it is in my nature.

Love is what you are—what *I am*.

Love is doing the things I like, saying the things I feel and creating smiles all around.
I am loving myself constantly.
I love myself.
I love you.

I am love.

We all are.

I love you.

21. BEING HUMAN

Wow!
I created myself on a planet called Earth.
I am a human being.
What an opportunity to experience the things created in this dimension of love!

I can be all that I want to be.
There are limitless possibilities to experience myself as Source, as love.
I am being human, and I am learning "being" more every day.

I have a beauty-full body, a mind to think, a spirit and a soul.
I am all that is, and as a human being, I experience the reflection of myself through all.

Being human is fun.
I love being on this planet.
I create myself as a human being that chooses love, evolution and joy.
I am a human being—being human on planet Earth.

There are many human beings all over the world.
While we all are special and unique, we all are one, and live in the same place.

It is great to be human.
I love being a human being like me.

I am a human being.

22. BEING ATTENTIVE

I am aware of all that happens around me and inside of me as well. I am attentive to the things I say, think and do. By being attentive, I choose wisely what I want to experience. Being attentive is fun.

I learn many things when I am attentive, and I teach many things when others are attentive. I am attentive to my feelings, and honor them all the time. With attention, I enjoy all beings around me.

I am very attentive right now.

I live here and now as a human being in this world.

I am attentive to my breathing.

I am attentive to a smile.

I am attentive.

Were you attentive to what I just said?

Be attentive.

Now!

I am attention.

23. RESPECTFULLY

With grand joy, I respect all human beings.
How can it be any other way, when I respect myself?

I respect other's feelings because I respect my own feelings.
I respect other's choices because I respect my own choices.
I respect all living beings because I respect my life as a human being.
I respect nature because I respect myself as nature.
I respect the love that you are because that is who I am as well.

I respect the moment I live in right now.
I respect all that is, and all that is not.

I am respect.

Respectfully,
Me!

24. LETTING GO

There are things that happen sometimes to me that I would like to last for-ever—like a hug from a friend, time to play with a special toy, or taking a vaca-tion to a place I really like.

I choose to enjoy them in the moment and to let go of the desire to keep hold of them in order to create more space for new things to happen to me that I like. I choose to let them go in my mind.

Sometimes there are things that I do not like at all: if someone doesn't share something with me, if I am not invited to a party, or if I did not go on the vaca-tion I wanted.

Then I remember to let go of my desires and expectations in order to create more space for the things I do like and in order to enjoy the good things in my life.

I choose to let go of judgments, desires and expectations.

Now, let go of this page, and go on to the next one...

I am the power of letting go.

25. THE POWER WITHIN

How "power-full" I am.
Inside me there is so much power, even more than a superhero!

The power of my heart is endless; it guides me to be clear about my choices and how best to use my wisdom wherever I go. My power within lets me know when I should be brave, and it lets me know how good it is to speak the truth.

The more I create truth in my life, the more powerful I become.

This power is great because it comes from inside my being.
It is available all the time, and my wisdom is the key to open it.

I am a powerful being who embraces this power with love, bliss and joy.
I celebrate my power within.

I am a powerful being.

26. BEAUTY

I am the power of beauty, and I have the power to see beauty in all things and all beings.

How beauty-full it is to smell the flowers,
Watch the birds in the sky,
See the ocean and its waves.

How full of beauty the beings that surround me.
Beauty has so many faces and forms. It is so creative…beauty is an artist.

How beauty-full all children are—all humans, all the living things on my planet Earth.
How full of beauty to know that *I exist.*

How beauty-full it is to see me reflected in all I see.

I am a beauty-full human being.
My thoughts and feelings are full of beauty.
Thinking positive is beauty-full too.

I am beauty.
I am you.

Hey, did you know you are full of beauty, too?

27. CHANGE

All things change.
I change each moment and each day.
I grow.
I change the way I think, sometimes—the things I choose and the things I like.

Change is everywhere.
I can see it very clearly in the seasons.
Spring changes into summer, summer into autumn, and autumn into winter.
The weather is constantly changing.

I can see changes in my body; my shoe size changes each time my feet grow.
My winter coat does not fit me from last year.
My fingers have outgrown my gloves.

Change is great!
Even my creation is changing, moment-to-moment, with my choices.

Did you know that there is only one thing in the whole universe that never changes?

Guess…

It is change itself!

I am the power of change

28. MIRACLES

All that I am is a miracle.
I am a wonderful and unique being.
I am even more than that!

A miracle is opening my eyes and seeing other miracles walking by.

I am a miracle—my legs, my arms, my heart, my head—my whole body is a miracle in itself.

Saying "I love you" is a miracle.
I create miracles all around.
With my smile I make others smile.

Earth is a miracle.
Love is a miracle.
Existence is a miracle in itself.

We all are a miracle—a miracle of love.

I am a miracle

29. YOU SAY WHAT I SAY

You say I am beautiful…well, so are you.
You say I make you smile…likewise.

You say I teach you so many things…well, likewise.
You like the things I like…likewise!

You want me to be happy…likewise.
You remind me of who I am…likewise.

The best part of it is that you love me just as I am…

We are one

30. MIRRORS

How amazing it is to see myself in everything.
How wonderful it is to recognize myself in so many things.

I see myself in nature.
I see myself in the sea.
I see myself in a bird flying.
I see myself in every living being.
I see myself in the clouds.
I see myself in the sky.

And where I like to see myself most
Is in the reflection of my own heart.

Mirror, mirror on the wall…did you know that everything is love?

I am a mirror of love.

31. HEALTHY LIMITS

Healthy limits assist me in growing as a person and as a whole human being. I honor my healthy limits. Healthy limits include respect, kindness, being selective, sometimes being quiet and sometimes speaking the truth. I set healthy limits with love and courage.

I respect myself and let others know they should respect me.
I speak the truth, and invite others to do the same.
I respect all living beings, and I like my life to be respected.
I say *"No"* when it is necessary, and *"Yes"* when it is necessary, too.

I never compromise the truth that I am...
This is a healthy limit.

My healthy limits have nothing to do with the limitless possibilities of love and kindness. The possibility of my creation is limitless. I set healthy limits that help me to grow in a balanced and loving environment.

The love for myself is limitless.

Life is good.

32. PLANET EARTH

I live on a beautiful planet; its name is Earth. I respect it, for it is my home; it is where I live. The wind that carries the oxygen that I breathe is part of my planet. I like the colors of my world, the animals, and the trees.

What a privilege to be here now, in this human form, living on a rich planet like Earth.

From my planet, I can see the moon, sun and stars.

I am creating positive thoughts to assist my universe in being clean, non-polluted and harmonious.

I love myself being here.

Planet Earth, thank you.
I love you as myself.

33. GRATITUDE

I am grateful for the air I breathe.
Thank you, oxygen.

I am grateful for the water I drink.
Thank you, thirst.

I am grateful to be alive.
Thank you, creation.

I am grateful to sing.
Thank you, song.

I am grateful to cry.
Thank you, tear.

I am grateful to hug.
Thank you, arms.

I am grateful to love.
Thank you, heart.

Thank you for the beings all around me.
Thank you for being me.

Thank you, me.

I am gratitude.

PART III
AFFIRMATIONS FOR PARENTS AND CHILDREN

o o o o o o o o o o o o o o o o o o o o o o o o o o o o o o

If my heart can become pure and simple
like that of a child,
I think there probably can be
no greater happiness than this.

—Kitaro Nishida

PART III
AFFIRMATIONS FOR PARENTS AND CHILDREN

These affirmations are very useful and very practical tools. Whenever you remember, you can repeat them. You can teach one or two to your children, but please do not overwhelm them! Remember that one is enough. Take one step at a time.

Let your children choose which affirmations they like, if possible. You can even write one down and decorate it in a colorful way and hang it on the wall in your child's room.

With my own daughter, I wrote the affirmations and she decorated them. We hung them on the wall (only five different ones to begin with) and believe me, she learned them and enjoyed them a lot. She even created a song about them.

Please interact with your children, explaining what these affirmations mean to you. Find ways to show your children "This is what it means." "This is who I am."

I've divided the affirmations into two groups: one set for parents and one for children. Although some are the same, they are created for the appropriate age and understanding of the child's mind. I was also very careful in selecting them so the Positive Parent can use their affirmations in a positive loving way, not as an egotistical boast.

I've used these affirmations many times with the children who attend my workshops, and they just love them. They can feel them and play with them (which is the best way of learning something in a fun, celebratory game). The parents that work with me in my meditation classes, too, feel empowered and confident, but mostly they feel love.

Enjoy these affirmations and use them wisely.

POSITIVE CHILD AFFIRMATIONS

I AM.

I AM ALIVE.

I AM AWARE.

I AM BEAUTIFUL.

I AM REAL.

I AM TRUTHFUL.

I AM GRATEFUL.

I AM RESPONSIBLE.

I AM UNIQUE.

I AM SMART.

I AM CONSTANT.

I AM PATIENT.

I AM SHARING.

I AM LOVING.

I AM COURAGEOUS.

I AM LIGHT.

I AM CARING.

I AM A MIRACLE.

I AM CREATING.

I AM SPECIAL.

I AM SILENT.

I AM LAUGHING.

I AM CELEBRATING.

I AM RESPECTFUL.

I AM CONFIDENT.

I AM TRUST.

POSITIVE PARENT AFFIRMATIONS

I AM.

I AM LIFE.

I AM CONSCIOUSNESS.

I AM BEAUTY.

I AM REALITY.

I AM TRUTH.

I AM GRATITUDE.

I AM RESPONSIBILITY.

I AM UNIQUENESS.

I AM WISDOM.

I AM CONSTANCY.

I AM PATIENCE.

I AM SHARING.

I AM LOVING.

I AM COURAGE.

I AM ENLIGHTENMENT.

I AM COMPASSION.

I AM A MIRACLE.

I AM CREATION.

I AM SPECIAL.

I AM SILENCE.

I AM LAUGHTER.

I AM CELEBRATION.

I AM RESPECTFUL.

I AM CONFIDENCE.

I AM TRUST.

POSITIVE CHILD AFFIRMATIONS

I AM ATTENTIVE.

I AM CHOOSING.

I AM WATCHING.

I AM POSITIVE.

I AM SMILING.

I AM PERSISTENT.

I AM YOU.

I AM ALL.

I AM POWERFUL.

I AM ONE.

I AM.

POSITIVE PARENT AFFIRMATIONS

I AM ATTENTION.

I AM A CHOICE.

I AM A WITNESS.

I AM POSITIVE.

I AM A SMILE.

I AM PERSISTENCE.

I AM YOU.

I AM ALL.

I AM EMPOWERMENT.

I AM ONENESS.

I AM.

PART IV
PRACTICAL EXERCISES
FOR THE POSITIVE CHILD

o o o o o o o o o o o o o o o o o o o o o o o o o o o o o o o o

I threw my cup away
when I saw a child drinking from his hands
at the trough.

—*Diogenes*

PART IV
PRACTICAL EXERCISES FOR THE POSITIVE CHILD

o o o o o o o o o o o o o o o o o o o o o o o o o o o o o o o o o

The Imaginative Child will become the imaginative man or woman most apt to invent, and therefore to foster, civilization.

—*Marcus Aurelius Antonius*

Here you will find ten exercises that you can use. Find the exercise that is most appropriate to the current situation you would like to assist your child with, or you may choose one that you may need for yourself. These exercises have worked beautifully for me with my own children and also for the children who attend my meditation classes.

I have found that these exercises have allowed children to feel more peaceful, to let go of hatred, to express unspoken words, to decrease nightmares and to feel more confident about themselves.

All that is needed is the assistance and consistency of Positive Parents to begin a magical journey through these practical exercises of love.

1. DRAWING EMOTIONS

o o o o o o o o o o o o o o o o o o o o o o o o o o o o o o o o o
In the middle of difficulty lies opportunity.

—*Albert Einstein*

Have four pieces of paper ready that are big enough to be able to stick on a wall for children to see. Choose appropriate colors for what you are going to draw.

You will draw four hearts.
  Draw the first one with a happy face.
  Draw the second one with a sad face.
  Draw the third one with an angry face.
  Draw the last one with no face so the children can choose a face of their own style to draw.

Show the children your drawings and say,
  "This is Mr. Happy Heart."
  "This is Mr. Sad Heart."
  "This is Mr. Angry Heart, and the last Mr. Heart is waiting for you to choose what face you would like him to have."

At the end of the exercise you can say, "No matter how each of these hearts choose to behave or choose to be; a heart is always a heart, just as you are always love."

With this exercise children not only learn names for their emotions, but also how their emotions look to others. They see the relationship between one emotion and the opposite emotion, then they have a choice as to what to do or not to do when situations arise.

The next time they experience any of the emotions you have drawn, a simple reminder, "Oh, I see you choose the same face as Mr. Happy Heart, or Mr. Sad Heart," will help them remember. You will be practicing with them the recognition of their emotions, and believe me, it will be very helpful for you, too. Just be gentle when reminding your children. Do not be intrusive. Be mindful to always use your Language of Love, respecting your child's space and their individuality.

2. THE PURPLE BUBBLE

o o o o o o o o o o o o o o o o o o o o o o o o o o o o o o o
The only thing that stands between a man and
what he wants from life is often merely
the will to try it and the faith to believe that it is possible.

—Richard M. DeVos

It happened. It was something I was not expecting to happen, but it did. It was the moment that nightmares descended upon my precious positive daughter's head! My heart ached.., but at the same time I decided to focus on the positive and I created this exercise for her. Now this visualization is used by many of her friends—and my friends, too. This exercise can be used not only for sleep time, but also during stressful times such as before your child goes to school or any time they are afraid. This exercise is helpful for anxiety, fear, upset, lack of confidence, or any separation feelings your child may be having.

Now, parents open your minds and read this with the power of your imagination.

"_____(Say your child's name), I love you. It is time to go to sleep (or go to school, or relax, or lie down). Let's blow, with your imagination, a big purple bubble. Let's blow a really big one together. Now imagine that you get inside your purple bubble. Inside your bubble there is fairy dust showering you with health, protection and love. Imagine all of this. Now that you are inside your bubble, you can go to sleep. There is no need to worry. This bubble won't pop until you wake up in the morning."

Ask your child if he or she would like to send purple bubbles to their friends or to any other member of the family with an intention (like love, peace, kindness, generosity, happiness, health) around them.

As your child gets more familiar with practicing this visualization you can ask them what they would like to have inside their bubble. It can be love, happiness, bliss, fun, or even their favorite toys. Remember, they are the ones who choose! Allow them to do the thinking.

After practicing this for a couple of days you might just need to remind your child when they get into bed, "Did you get inside of your bubble already?" You could also ask, "Do you want to create your bubble this time by yourself?" That may be all that is required for them to experience a restful sleep.

3. A LETTER OF LOVE

o o o o o o o o o o o o o o o o o o o o o o o o o o o o o o o o o

Love one another but make not a bond of love.

Let there be a moving sea between the shores of your souls.

Sing and dance together and be joyous,

but let each one of you be alone.

—Kahlil Gibran

This exercise is used for letting go of sadness, expressing emotions, creating a mood of acceptance, and experiencing self-worth. It also allows children to express their feelings in a whole new way. This exercise could also be called *the moment of truth*. If your child already knows how to write, let them write the letter of love themselves.

I created this exercise for my daughter because she used to come home from school saying things like,

"Mommy, that boy hit me."

"That girl doesn't want to play with me."

"That boy did not invite me to his party."

"My friend is upset; what should I do?"

You, as a parent, must have had to listen to one or maybe a couple of these examples from your own child. Haven't you? I said to her, "Okay, my love, we are going to let your friends know how you are feeling and what you would like to create—or what you would like to have happen instead."

There is no exact format for this exercise. The only instruction I have is, "Remember, this is a letter that is written respectfully, with kind words and gentle feelings." Then I recommend beginning the letter with "In the name of love" and sign the letter with the words, "In the name of love, I am love." (That way, we reinforce positive values and feelings of love in our children). While your child writes the letter or dictates what you should write in their letter, you can help them choose various options for words that might be disrespectful or unkind. Again, please give your child options, rather than simply shaming them by harshly saying, "*No*, that is not an appropriate word!" Remember, if you want the positive, you need to give the positive, because if that is the language you choose, you might find the next letter your son or daughter will write may be for you!

In our house, I created a homemade mailbox for our bookcase into which my children can mail their letters to me. If you decide to do that, too, then any time your child writes a letter to you they can put it in the box. If they express feelings of being upset or sad, acknowledge their feelings and see this as a gift.

Wouldn't you rather have your children express their emotions and put them inside a cardboard box instead of keeping those emotions inside their minds, and later, as grown ups, manifest those strong emotions in other negative ways? Perhaps you know what I mean…

You and your children can create letters for any type of situation or emotion—for the negative times and also for the positive, celebratory times. Maybe they wish to say "thank you" or to show you that they are grateful. You can even have your children write to Mother Earth, God, the ocean, an animal, or other family members.

Follow your heart and do this exercise yourself. When the letter is finished, place it in an envelope, close it, draw or stick a stamp on it and put it in the box and let it go. If a child can do it himself, let him do it. If you have a younger child, put it in the box with her and say good-bye to the letter.

In the name of love, I would like to share with you a few letters written by students at my mediation classes for children.

Letter of Love #1
Written by Paco, seven years old

Dear Daniel,
In the name of love, I want to tell you that I got very mad because you did not give me your new truck. My mommy says that the truck is yours…but also I heard my mommy saying the other day to my sister that she should share her doll with Adriana. Next time I see you, I am going to ask my mommy to tell you to share. When I play with your truck, I will share it with you.

In the name of love, I am love.
Paco

Letter of Love #2
Written by Susana's Mommy
Dictated by Susana, almost three years old

Dear Daddy,
In the name of love, I want to tell you that I cried at night because you are not here. I punched my mommy in the face and mommy got upset. I miss you. I use the potty now.

In the name of love, I am love.
Susana

Letter of Love #3
Written by Eduardo, forty-three years old
To: Eduardo, six years old

Dear Son,
In the name of love, I want to tell you how special you are for me. How happy my heart feels to know that you are alive! I want to tell you that I sometimes get upset, but I never get upset at you. I love you and I always will.

In the name of love,
Dad

Letter of Love #4
Written to *The Positive Child* Reader

Dear Positive Child Reader,
In the name of love, I want to share with you my gratitude for reading these words and my salutations to your interest in becoming a better human being and a more loving parent each day. I celebrate your journey with you and invite you to share your beautiful heart with your children and with the world.

In the name of love,
Ivonne Delaflor

4. HITTING A PILLOW

o o o o o o o o o o o o o o o o o o o o o o o o o o o o o o o
An eye for an eye makes the whole world blind.

—Mohantas K. Gandhi

This is a simple exercise for the times when you or your children are so angry that you or they would like to hit walls, slam doors and break things. Often children even wish to smash the special new toy you bought for them that they wanted so much! If these moments happen in your house with your children or with yourself, talk to them about this exercise when they are calm. Then the next time that your child begins with a burst of energy (I choose to label it that), quickly get two pillows (yes, *two* pillows), and say to your child, "From now on, when moments like this happen in this house we will take a pillow and begin hitting it." Then hold the pillow and demonstrate to your child how to do it!

In the beginning, my daughter would hit the pillow very strongly and bite it intensely. As time passed, she began to "grow out of" the need to hit things and she preferred not to do that. As soon as I ran for the pillow, she would usually scream for a moment and then decide to stop!

Of course this is a "*do it only in your own home*" *exercise*! Be sure your children understand this boundary. Really make sure! Sometimes I've heard parents say to me that they have used this technique, but that their children began to hit grandma's pillow or the pillow of someone else when they were visiting a friend. Let them know that some people might not understand about hitting a pillow instead of throwing things or breaking things and may become angry or upset if they choose to do this exercise away from home.

5. I AM A LION

o o o o o o o o o o o o o o o o o o o o o o o o o o o o o o o o o o o
We don't see things as they are; we see them as we are.

—*Anais Nin*

With this exercise, our Positive Child not only uses the power of his or her imagination, but also finds an appropriate and acceptable environment in which to scream and shout. I use this when children are screaming a lot or getting into quarrels. I am sure you can find other uses for this technique to diffuse a child's natural outbursts of energy.

When I sense the situation between children is about to get out of control, I usually shout, "Lion Time!" Then I scream, "AAAAAAAAAAAAAAAAhhhhh— here come the lions!" Then the children begin to crawl around the floor (or grass or patio) and the powerful roaring starts. Within five minutes your children will have had the screaming dose that they've needed and they will be ready for some quiet time.

Remember to remind your little lions, however, that they are a special type of lion that doesn't bite, but that they have the most powerful roars in the "Home Jungle."

I've also used this game to invite my children to lunch by just calling, "Where are the lions? Their food is served!" They come roaring to the kitchen. You should see it—they eat like lions, too! By the way, you might need to remind these lions that they need to use silverware! Just in case they forget.

6. IMAGINING THE VOICE AS A RADIO

○ ○
As I grow older,
I pay less attention to what men say.
I just watch what they do.

—Andrew Carnegie

Sometimes when children turn their "volume voices" up and we need quiet, we don't know what to do. Regularly, parents will scream back to their child, *"Be quiet! You are speaking too loudly!"* It is often hard to remember that what we ask for we should model, otherwise it is a waste of energy, a creation of more turmoil, and we are not congruent with what we think, say and do. Our children learn from our example. As the Positive Parent that we are in this and all exercises, if we speak quietly, our children will model that. For children to learn about silence and lowering their voices they must have that demonstrated in a fun way. You can speak to your child and have a serious conversation about silence and quiet. I trust they will understand. Keep it simple, and in the process nurture your own Positive Child within.

The power of imagination in children is grand. One day six-year-old Danna was screaming at her mother, "I don't want to brush my hair today." The screaming became louder and louder. Theresa, Danna's mom, was beginning to lose her patience until her own imagination and a helpful deep breath created this idea. She said, "Danna" (say the name of your child to capture her whole attention), "in this moment I am imagining that my voice is a radio." You would use this word—imagining—keeping reality in its place and being truthful regarding the fact that the voice is simply the voice.

Danna said, "What? That can't be! You are not a radio."

Theresa replied, "Yes, I am. I am imagining I am a radio. My left ear is the button to turn me off and my right ear controls the volume. My nose changes the radio stations. My mouth is the speaker where the songs come out. Let me show you."

Theresa began playing with her imagination. She pushed her nose and her voice began singing different tunes. The more she pushed her nose and changed the stations; many tunes began to play—sung by mommy, of course! When she began playing favorite songs of Danna's, she said, "I think the volume is too low.

Let me turn it up." Danna was now exited and happy and learning about *VOICE VOLUME* in a natural, fun and appropriate way for her age.

When they finished playing the voice radio, Theresa asked her daughter, "Could you use your voice volume to tell me what type of brush you are going to choose to brush your hair with?" Theresa gave her daughter two positive options, instead of going back and reminding the child that she was screaming just a few minutes ago. She kept the statement in the present time. Danna answered in a very low voice, *"the pink one."*

Theresa said, "Excuse me, I didn't hear you." Then Danna turned the volume button up and began to speak. Theresa told her, "That is too loud! Could you please lower the volume?" Danna did.

Through play, a lesson of quiet was given. Theresa is not a psychologist or a child specialist. She is just a mom who looked within her own Positive Child nature and allowed that wisdom to create a beautiful moment, which manifested itself through patience, compassion and the language of Love.

7. FLOWER POWER
The Positive TIME-OUT Alternative

o o o o o o o o o o o o o o o o o o o o o o o o o o o o o o

View all problems as challenges.

Look upon negativities that arise as opportunities to learn and to grow.

Don't run from them, condemn yourself, or bury your burden in saintly silence.

You have a problem?

Great. More grist for the mill.

Rejoice, dive in, and investigate.

—*Bhante Henepola Gunaratana,*
"Mindfulness in Plain English"

For this exercise, find a special beautiful place in your home—an open space and a nice comfortable chair with a plant or a flower close by. My six-year old daughter has a comfortable puffy "flower" chair. This chair is in the living room, close to a window where a lot of light comes through. It is in front of a beautiful plant. When my daughter is angry or screaming her way out of things toward someone in the family, or just very tired, she goes to sit in her flower. One day I noticed that she liked to do that, so I asked her why. She told me it was nice to talk to her plant when she was upset. We all agreed that that particular spot would be called "Flower Power" and that when anyone—including Daddy or Mommy—was upset or felt like yelling, we would go and sit in the Flower Power.

This has been on amazing point of focus for all of us. Sometimes it works; sometimes it doesn't, but the focus and positive option to direct our anger there is what is important. This is a great alternative to the *TIME OUT* concept that is always associated with punishment, as a time to think about "what you did wrong." This is a positive way of saying to our children that a whole range of emotions are okay, and that mastering the mind by thinking positively is a practice. They will also experience that there is a positive option for letting our "angries" out.

The most important part of this is the modeling! Model the emotions that you want your children to learn, and be honest. Next time you lose control or anger gets in the way of the clarity of what you intend to say, then run, breathe and sit in your Flower Power. Charge yourself with intention, focus and love to redirect the situation in the most loving and respectful way. Practicing intention and focus will assist your child to be aware of his own thoughts and feelings. We must *model* the experience, however!

The intention is not to *force your child* to do something else. He must choose to go to the Flower Power himself! It must be an internal choice. At the beginning, of course, if your child is angry and you suggest going to Flower Power, she/he might not like it. Instead, you can walk silently and sit in Flower Power, breathing quietly. You might also speak out loud to direct the experience. "I feel angry now." (Please do not say, "*I am angry!*" This is important, because who we *are* is not affected by our emotions. *I am* remains intact and it is not a positive affirmation to reaffirm in the subconscious.) Then you can continue and say, "I will take three deep breaths and remain silent for a moment." That is all that is needed. Stay in the Flower Power for five minutes. Your child may still be screaming or doing his/her thing; hold on, remain centered, and remember that you are modeling a positive alternative. Remember, we create our realities, and if you can guide your children to realize that within themselves, then their true Flower Power will blossom and grow!

8. I LIKE YOU AND...GAME

○ ○
Why not try and see positive things,
to just touch those things and make them bloom?

—Thich Nhat Hanh

When we go shopping or are at a social event, we behave as perfect parents and polite human beings. We often put labels of perfection on others, forgetting the label we add to ourselves, yet rarely do we take the time to look eye to eye with our children and let them know what we like about them. Do we tell our children how special they are? I'm not referring to letting them know what we like that about their actions—how well they sit at the table for meals or how they are being quiet when that is expected, or using their good manners to speak to others. Have you told your children lately that they are unique human beings?

In the exercise, address your child and tell them how much you like them, without adding any labels or reasons. "*I like you*" connotes wholeness. It includes everything that one is. We may describe the action we like, but maintain the fact that *I like you* is a complete statement of your unconditional love.

A few minutes a day to connect with your child will be sufficient. Separating your expectations of what you want your children to become with who they *are* can assist us in lifting the veil between those very different aspects. Choose to have a peek into who you child really is and who they came to earth to be.

I have recommended the following practice to my friends. Here is an example of how one person uses it with her five-year-old child. It is a simple exercise to reaffirm our self-esteem and maintain our awareness of the amazing wisdom and purity of our positive children.

Maria noticed that she usually praised everyone she encountered with positive words. "That's a lovely dress." "Great hair!" "I really like your car." One day she became aware that only rarely did she say nice things to her son, Ramón. She would praise him for his good grades at school or his polite manner when eating at the table, but that was all. That evening Maria understood that those things were not enough. A question arose in her mind that she shared with me. "Is my child just the well-behaved person I see, or is my son a human being who has more to show me about who he truly is?"

I suggested to her to consider the *I like you and…exercise*. I recommended that she choose a specific time when Ramón's play would not be interrupted. It was important that her intention be full of love, rather than rushing or doing many things at the same time. Maria began practicing the game every morning before taking Ramón to school. She decided to use only a few words to address the unique qualities in the persona of her son. She set a limit to the words and at the beginning and the end of the exercise, she chose to say, *"I love you."* She also invited Ramón to play the same game with her. Here is how it went.

Maria:

> I love you, Ramón.
> I like you and how you treat your dog with kindness.
> I like you and how your eyes shine when you see the stars.
> I like you and I love to listen to you sing alone in your room with such a powerful voice.
> I like you, and your quiet ways remind me to lower my voice.
> I love you, Ramón.

Then Ramón had his turn.

> I love you, Mommy.
> I like you, and you are my mommy.
> I like you and you give me hugs.
> I like you and your kisses
> I love you, Mommy, and I love you.

As a simple gesture of love and acceptance, this exercise can be a fulfilling reminder for both parent and child in just a few moments everyday.

9. I SPEAK A NEW LANGUAGE

o o o o o o o o o o o o o o o o o o o o o o o o o o o o o o o o

Imagine there's no heaven. It's easy if you try.

No hell below us; above us only sky.

Imagine all the people, living for today.

—John Lennon

This game is for a parent to initiate. It promotes active listening, attention and the ability to be present in the moment.

The other day I was trying to explain to my daughter that calling people names was not an option for her. I tried all my skills as a Parent Talk Trainer, as a meditation teacher, as a mommy, and nothing had worked. The more I spoke, the more she screamed and yelled words and names. I'm sure you can imagine the scenario!

Suddenly I began speaking like this: "Aruybuduba dabab baada a poropoprop lahate hh hrh acataca acataca trucu?"

I created my own language, and oh, what a miracle! My daughter stopped screaming and asked, "What are you doing?"

"It's my new language for you. I want you to understand that we can't call people names."

Then she said, "Oh, I get it." Then she finished her sentence, "Badabada!"

10. COLORFUL DANCE

o o o o o o o o o o o o o o o o o o o o o o o o o o o o o o o o o

Go as far as you can see and when you get there,
you will always be able to see farther.

—Zig Ziglar

This exercise is helpful for promoting creativity and individuality, establishing peace of mind and recognizing emotions. When it is used with the body to paint, with both feet and hands, it also incorporates rhythm. This exercise gives a child a sense of loving their human body. It therefore increases acceptance of self, and at the same time it offers a colorful experience of reality.

Find a safe space in which your children can paint. Have available some non-toxic paints that can also be used for finger painting. Have at least four different colors and some cups or bowls or containers to pour the color into and one for water as well. Have big pieces of paper placed all around the area you've chosen to paint in.

What I've found is that children like to choose some old clothes to wear every time they paint. My daughter has her "painter" uniform and it is already full of color and rainbows and hearts! We never wash it; it is her creation.

Now, set a healthy limit by explaining to the children what the appropriate painting area is. Tell them that if anyone chooses to go outside those limits, that will be the end of their painting session. In this way, you are setting guidelines for them while promoting choices, limits and responsibility for what happens.

Now it is time to paint! I like to play music—either salsa, or mambo—music that makes you want to celebrate and delight in the process of creation. When I choose energetic music, we usually paint with our knees, feet, and elbows. We dance all over the paper and have fun, trying to follow the rhythm of the music without forcing anyone to dance. Remember, each child has a choice. There are times when I want to create a more relaxed experience of painting. Then I choose some Bach or some Mozart to set the mood.

Try to participate with your children in the process of creating visual art. You may find that it enlivens the child within you. There have been times when I've accompanied seven or eight children painting at the same time. It sometimes happens that one child will try to paint on another child's paper. Sometimes they like the drawing of another child better. When that happens, especially when mambo music is on, I invite everybody to dance all over everyone's papers, promoting sharing and letting go of the personal "mine." Usually, that is readily accepted by all. If not, make any adjustments necessary so each child's needs are heard and acknowledged.

Make sure to set healthy limits right at the beginning, with grand respect and love. If each child is going to have only one paper to paint on, make sure they know that. If you want them all to share one large sheet of paper, let them know that as well. Setting limits will make this colorful experience a time for celebration—a magical time, a time for love, rather than tears, competition and disappointment.

11. THE PATIENCE SEED

o o o o o o o o o o o o o o o o o o o o o o o o o o o o o o o o o

I know of no more encouraging fact than the unquestionable
ability of man to elevate his life by conscious endeavor.

—*Henry David Thoreau*

This is a special exercise to share with your children, because to plant a tree, flowers or a green plant is to provide a service for our planet. It also assists our children in understanding how things are created, how things mature, what ingredients are necessary in order for a seed to grow—things like love, food, water, caring, nurturing, and so on. However, it also promotes the responsibility of taking care of a seed or plant, while encouraging observation and being attentive to the subtle changes of *creation*. You and your child can watch the miracle of evolution together.

For this exercise, plant some seeds in your garden and keep a picture diary of the evolution of the seeds. While this is happening, explain the process to your child. In addition, tell him that with this seed you will both watch the creation of a miracle called "life"!

Share the responsibility of watering the growing plant with your child. Take turns and encourage your child to speak to the plant. It is scientifically proven that plants grow better when people talk to them and when they are feeling cared for. Give a name to the seed (or if you bought a plant, give that a name) so your child can feel connected with "Joey the Bean Plant" or "Adele the Apple Tree." Your child will develop their nurturing energy and at the same time serve by creating more plants that give oxygen to our precious world.

As a bonus, you will give your child the opportunity to practice patience! Whenever they ask, "When will it sprout?" or "When will it bloom?" with grand respect, answer them. "Have patience. We will be watching the evolution of this plant as it grows." By the way, while your children practice patience, why not practice it yourself? See, there is always a great opportunity in everything we do!

Just watch. Be loving, be patient just love!

12. CALLING BROTHER LOVE

o o o o o o o o o o o o o o o o o o o o o o o o o o o o o o o o o
Keep your face to the sunshine and you cannot see the shadows.

—*Helen Keller*

This one is a beautiful, simple exercise that you can do wherever you are.

Whenever your child is crying, has gotten hurt, is feeling sad or has had a nightmare—whatever the experience is—you can offer them this because your heart just wants to give them love.

When my children have fallen down and hurt themselves, or have had a strong dream, I help them by calling "Brother Love" to assist us. Here is an example you can use as a model.

"_____(Fill in your child's name), let's close our eyes for a moment while placing your hand on your heart, for with our imagination we can pretend that this is the phone to contact Brother Love or My Friend Love or Doctor Love or Sister Love—respecting whatever name your child feels most comfortable with. Now, let's dial with our breath his phone number and tell me when he responds!" It is important to wait for your child to say, "Yes I feel it!"

You might want to ask softly, "Do you feel him?" if the child's response takes a long time.

"Now tell Brother Love what is happening for you in this moment in a quiet way, and listen to what Brother Love has to say to you."

Next, ask your child if he or she would like to share what Brother Love said. If your child does, you will be surprised by their sweet responses. If they don't want to share it with you, let it still be a surprise and a sweet response as well.

My daughter told me one day, after asking what Brother Love said to her, that "Brother Love said that he will heal you, too."

My response to her was, "*Wow!* and *Mega Wow!* Thank you!"

13. FEEDING MY DOG

o o o o o o o o o o o o o o o o o o o o o o o o o o o o o o o o o

Let us not be content to wait and see what will happen,
but give us the determination to make the right things happen.

—*Peter Marshall*

This exercise is most appropriate with a little dog as a pet. (It doesn't work as well with a fish or a frog.) Dogs grow up and learn what we teach them, and as they grow, they become part of the family. This is a very helpful exercise to use as a model for your children to learn the importance of love, nurturing, limits and respect.

I always advise parents that if they are going to get a pet for their children, to do it when the child is old enough to walk the dog, clean up their poop, and really take care of a pet, not when the child is only three or four years old. For the sake of family harmony and a positive emotional expression, be aware of the right time to introduce a pet into your lives. Appropriate timing is a skill that a Positive Parent knows very well. If the timing is not right, then the only thing that you might hear in the house is blame: "This is your dog! Clean this mess up or I'll give your dog away!"

Before your child is gifted with a pet, it is a good idea to require them to learn by heart this Responsibility Prayer:

I will be responsible for my new pet,
Feeding his body with his food and feeding his spirit with my love.
I will make sure he eats twice a day.
I will make sure to treat him with respect.
I will walk my dog for him to pee.
While I walk, I'll be attentive also to me.
I will clean the mess my doggy makes.
I will wash my hands after that.
I will have grand patience.
And will practice to be the best positive trainer,
To have a well-behaved puppy always with me.

So now, you just picked out a new doggy that your seven or eight-year-old child has been begging for. You have already spoken to your child about the responsibilities regarding their dog. They have learned the Responsibility Prayer and you've created a contract that you will hang up on the refrigerator. (Please give a copy to your child as well)

Here is an example of a simple contract: "Healthy Limit Scroll," or whatever the name you want to choose for setting responsible limits.

I will walk my dog at least once a day.
I will feed him and pet him daily.
I will clean up any mess that he makes.
I will bathe him when he needs it.
I will make sure he is clean, happy and receives lots of love.

This is a simple way to reinforce being responsible and to show your child how to nurture and care for someone who depends on you. It also demonstrates the importance of boundaries to children. In addition, it offers an experience of having responsibilities, just like parents do.

PART V
BUMPER STICKERS
AND DAILY QUOTES

○ ○
Children: One Earthly thing truly experienced,
even once, is enough for a lifetime.

—Rilke

PART V
BUMPER STICKERS FOR THE POSITIVE CHILD WITHIN

I have created these quotes to share with the parents of my meditation classes to remind them of their child within. I believe that if you can't remember to play, to trust and to love with the confidence of a child, then it will be very hard to really tap into the universe of your children.

Parents at my class created bumper stickers, shared them with friends and with their children, too. Here is one of my favorites:

More Positive Thinking, More Love and More Play!

Remember, the more often you repeat these quotes as affirmations, the more quickly you *become* them.

I am a Positive Parent and a Positive Child as well!

DAILY QUOTES TO BE USED AS BUMPER STICKERS

1.
I am a child of God, I am…I live, I breathe.
I am alive!
I AM.

2.
As I play, I remember that it is a miracle
Being Human!
I AM A MIRACLE.

3.
My tears are beautiful.
My laughter is powerful.
My heart is beating…
God lives in my soul.
I AM BEAUTIFUL.

4.
I am protected.
I follow my heart.
Just like the day
Follows the night.
I AM THE WAY.

5.
The games I choose to play
Assist me in reminding my parents
That they shall play as well.
I AM PLAYFUL.

6.
I learn, I teach and then I learn again.
I AM LEARNING.
I AM A STUDENT OF LOVE.

7.
Like a bubble full of wonder
Is my joy and so is my laughter.
I AM JOY.

8.
I always remember that I am a child…
And a very responsible one.
I AM RESPONSIBILITY.

9.
When I watch the sunset, I remember
God created it for me. I AM GRATITUDE.

10.
The fragrance of a flower reminds me
That my fragrance is my soul.
I AM ONENESS.

11.
If a bubble can pop,
A sad thought can pop, too.
I AM CREATING MY REALITY.

12.
I laugh.
I sing.
I dance.
I am.
I AM LAUGHTER.

13.
My favorite game I play is with a smile on my face.
I AM SMILING.

14.
When there is rain in the sky,
The flowers are being bathed by God.
I AM AWARE.

15.
The snow comes to play with the trees
While I go to play with the snow.
This is sharing.
I AM SHARING.

16.
A doll, a car, a plane or a teddy bear...
A kiss, a tear, a hug or my mom...
All of these are created by God.
I AM WATCHING.

17.
My friends, the sky, the stars, the clouds
Are always with me wherever I am.
I AM ABUNDANCE.

18.
I dream, I play, I cry, I laugh.
This is being human,
This is called life!
I AM UNITY IN DIVERSITY.

19.
I take care of my body,
As I take care of the plants.
I take care of the ocean,
As I take care of my heart!
I AM CARING.

20.
I think about health.
I speak about health.
A flower is healthy with water.
I am healthy with my own breath.
I AM HEALTH.

21.
I can choose to play.
I can choose to sing.

I can choose to express
The love I feel for me.
I AM THE POWER OF CHOICE.

22.
I believe in life.
I believe in love.
I believe in me.
I believe in trust.
I AM TRUTH.

23.
The rain celebrates the presence of the clouds.
My planet celebrates my presence through my heart.
I AM CELEBRATION.

24.
What is yesterday?
What is the future?
What is the present?
It is all time.
I AM HERE AND NOW.

25.
Just as my planet gives me the food I eat every day,
There are beings that I serve in whatever way I can.
I AM KINDNESS.

26.
In whatever job I have,
And whoever I meet there,
I am glad to be alive.
And remember I can breathe. I AM CONTENTMENT.

27.
A parent of God I am.
As I am more aware of this,
I create more love in my life.
I AM AWARENESS.

28.
Obstacles, difficulties, sadness or tears,
Hatred, judgments, illusions or fears…
I give no power to these…
For I am always aware
That my child within will know what to choose and say.
I AM POSITIVE.

29.
Children are a gift.
They remind me of who I am…
Through a whisper, through a tear, through their sleepy eyes at night.
I AM REMEMBRANCE.

30.
I choose to play while alive.
I choose to love while awake.
I choose to enjoy my children
And enjoy myself in the same way.
I AM READY.

31.
Thank you, sweet existence.
Thank you, sweetest earth.
Thank you for the opportunity
To be a positive child again!
I AM A POSITIVE PARENT-CHILD!
YES.

PART VI
PRACTICAL WISDOM
FOR THE POSITIVE PARENT

o o o o o o o o o o o o o o o o o o o o o o o o o o o o o o o o o o

Teach us to delight in simple things,
And mirth that has no bitter springs;
Forgiveness free of evil done,
And love to all men 'neath the sun.

—*Rudyard Kipling*

PART VI
PRACTICAL WISDOM FOR THE POSITIVE PARENT

This next section includes excerpts from the Positive Child Monthly Newsletters that the Mastery of Life Organization shares freely with anyone interested. The organization's main intention is to awaken the inner wisdom of Love that we all have, which easily expresses itself when joy, Positive Thinking and awareness of the present moment are the daily focus on our lives. These are wisdom tools for "Parenting from the Soul."

1. POSITIVE CHOICE

o o o o o o o o o o o o o o o o o o o o o o o o o o o o o o o o o o

Effective positive thinking requires adopting a positive attitude, perseverance in spite of difficulties or failures, positive words, positive actions, positive feelings, visualizing positively the outcome of whatever you do, having unwavering faith in yourself and your abilities, an inner attitude of success.

—*The Daily Guru*

What is the difference between a positive and a negative attitude? *A choice!* Being positive does not mean that you allow your children to do whatever they want without setting healthy limits for them. Yesterday a very good friend said to me, "Love doesn't mean that I am going to give my children everything they want."

Another mother confided in me, "I've been trying to be positive, as you say. Every day I remember that I have a choice: Either I can choose to feel either grumpy or joyful. As soon as I wake up and decide to feel joyful, though, something usually happens. Maybe my husband chooses to be in a grumpy mood or my children have a tantrum. So I begin to change my mood to please them with what *they* want, instead of creating the mood that I wanted to live that day, but it usually doesn't turn out that way."

A positive attitude is not altered by external situations—even the most extreme or painful ones. A positive choice remains, in spite of someone's tantrum, a "bad" day or an unexpected situation. Choosing to be, think and behave positively is and becomes a way of life—one's lifestyle. The reverberation of the constancy of thinking positively begins to permeate your surroundings: children, husband, wife, workplace, friends, and so on.

Being positive is a *choice*—a very useful one. It is a powerful reminder as to what words to say, how to direct our love to our children and to our partner, and how to guide our children in ways that empower their inner positive essence rather than coercing or just inputting our negative demands on them.

A child is positive by birthright. Without knowing the concept of *positive,* a child's attitude is already one of joy, of acceptance, and of adventure in discovering life. Every step of the way in a child's adventure—evolving, learning, playing, growing—they are all included. You can guide them through their mistakes and the possible choices they can make. Walk with them. Share, transmit and project your experience of life to them and leave a footstep in their soul.

Who do you choose to be when you are with your child?
Who do you choose to be in every situation?
Can you remember that *all* that you do, feel, or think is a choice?
Will you choose to remember that?

The next time you feel negative or in a state of distraction, anger, frustration, or aggression towards the ones you love (specifically your children), go quickly into your mind and ask yourself:
Is this really necessary?
Is there any other option?
How will my words impact my children?
How will my actions impact my children?

Some people say, "There is nothing I can do. My mind just takes over!" If this is the case for you or if it is your choice to believe that, try to remember that you are the one who selects your thoughts. Who is the one that uses your mind? Is your mind running wild? Are you choosing your mind to maintain the direction you want, through compassion, healthy limits and love? As always, it is your choice. You *can* do it.

2. WHO AM I?

o o o o o o o o o o o o o o o o o o o o o o o o o o o o o o o o o o o
I am the one that loves,
I am the one that feels,
I am the one that plays…I am simply me.

—Ivonne Delaflor

How many times have you said to your child,

"Don't be rude!"
"You are not nice!"
"You are not a good girl."
"You are not a good boy."
"Good boys or girls are not like that!"

It amazes me to see how we all get confused as to who we are through this lack of awareness in the way we talk and perceive reality. Your children *are not* their personality. We, as parents, must learn to see the real child, and not the habits, tendencies or behaviors that are part of the personality that accompanies their humanness.

Who we are is untouched by our personality. If we are a lawyer, that is not who we are; that is the activity or the work we choose to perform. If we feel hurt, angry or upset, that is not who we are either. Being upset, hurt or angry are attitudes or emotional responses to a situation!

Yes, all of these things are part of who we are—the personality we live with—but if we truly want our children to choose wisely and choose to be positive, we must embrace them as they are, not as who we want them to be. Children are not their behavior. If you ask your child to change a behavior that is not positive, an action that is disrespectful or that does not bring harmony to your family environment, then address your child with your Language of Love. Make it very clear that what you don't like is their behavior, but that you love *who they are* very much.

How can we empower our children to choose for themselves a Positive Personality? If we have a constant reminder for us as parents that our children are Love, and that their personality is being built by experiences, information, and imitation. Who we *are* remains always present. The self has a personality, but we are more than personality. We must always remember that.

First, you must be aware of who *you* are. Are you a lawyer or the person that chooses to be a lawyer? Are you a spiritual leader or a person who chooses that activity? Are you a mother, or a human being who chooses to bring beautiful souls into the world? Be very aware as a human being of *who* you are. Who is the one that feels? Is it you or the programming that says you are just like your mother? Is it you or the data that says you are negative and bad? Who you *are* remains pure and still in your heart of hearts. Who you are is the radiant, loving human being you see your children imitating. First, remember this in yourself. Then guide your children to remember this as well. It is so limiting to label children by their personality, and it's frustrating for them, too.

How would our world be different if parents would listen to their hearts and would stop behaving or acting from their own negative programming?

The other day in my meditation classes a child spit on one of the teachers. The teacher, aware of the importance of the Language of Love, said to the child, "That behavior you chose is better done in the sink when you brush your teeth, rather than on my body."

As the teacher was saying this, the mother was saying, "Bad boy, dirty boy!" The more the mother yelled at the child, the more he continued to spit!

This was a very simple response to a common occurrence, but this sensitive teacher addressed the situation and offered an important lesson to the mother. This boy stopped spitting on the teacher, but I heard he is still spitting on his mother…I wonder why?

Be very attentive as to who you are in order to respect who your children are as well. Constantly ask yourself, "Is this who I am? Am I the angry father, or is this a behavior that I must address in order to become less angry and let my real self resolve the situation in a calmer and wiser way? Am I the impatient mother? Am I a bad mother because I am impatient? Is this the way I must be aware that I am creating a difficult situation in my life?

Constantly remind yourself about these judgments, and I assure you that the next time your child does something you consider to be not an acceptable or healthy behavior, you will be ready to guide your child to choose a more positive situation through your wisdom, your awareness and of course, through the power of your Love.

3. DON'T RUSH

○ ○

Breathe and breathe some more...

—Donald Schnell

Have you ever considered the impact that choosing to be in a hurry has on your children?

Listen to this conversation:

"Alex, hurry up! We are going to be late!"
"But mommy, I need to brush my teeth."
"You can brush your teeth later. I don't have time to wait for you. I am late!"
"But I need to brush my hair, at least."
"You can do that in the car! Come on, hurry up!"

This is a situation that is repeated over and over again. It is said that if you want to learn something, practicing it will make an expert of you. Guess what? We are sending the message to our children with our hurry and impatience that it is okay to be late. We are saying that it is okay not to finish an activity or complete a responsibility that we have. We are supporting the idea that it is okay to put important things off until later.

Please remember that when your children are teenagers, you will want them to be able to dress appropriately, brush their teeth, finish their work, be on time, be truthful, be responsible, choose healthy food, be selective with their friends, believe in themselves, and be conscious that they create their own reality. Wow! What are we doing?

Dearest Positive Parents,

I invite you to take time and create time for yourself not to rush. Your children need to see your responsibility and patience because these qualities are going to be very necessary in future situations in their life.

The most refined skill some adults have is procrastination. Do you want your child to choose to model this type of behavior?

"I'll do it tomorrow."
"Leave it like that and I'll finish it later."
"I don't want to handle this problem now; I feel too tired."

A Positive Parent knows how to wait. A Positive Parent knows how to guide their children with consistency and healthy boundaries. A Positive Parent knows that practicing good deeds creates good deeds. A Positive Parent knows that patience carries within it grand wisdom. A Positive Parent knows that Love and the expression of it is worth ten million universes for the growth and evolution of our children.

Here is a story for you. Mary was in a rush. She was late for work and her son Daniel was not ready yet for school. She could have woken up earlier, but she chose to sleep in for ten more minutes that day, which then turned out to be thirty minutes. In her rush and bad temper, she screamed to Daniel, "If you are not ready in three minutes for school, I will leave you here by yourself!" Daniel started crying. He didn't know if his mother was telling the truth or not. His mother was getting more impatient, until Daniel, in the midst of his tears said to her, "Its okay, Mommy. If you leave me here, I will wait for you to come home again."

Mary's heart melted and realized that nothing was really *that* important to rush for. She realized that he thought she would leave him alone, that it was not just a hollow threat. She decided that day to begin to be responsible and tell her boss that she was late because of her decision. She took the time to dress Daniel, to kiss him and hug him, and when they were finally ready to go Daniel said to her, "Thank you, Mommy! Next time I will wake you up earlier with a big kiss."

My advice is *do not rush!* Stop *procrastinating!* Remember that your Positive Child is learning from you every minute of every day through your own modeled behavior. Relax, breathe and enjoy your children in the present, for tomorrow is already gone!

4. THE "E" WORD

o o o o o o o o o o o o o o o o o o o o o o o o o o o o o o o o o
Education is when you read the fine print.
Experience is what you get if you don't.

—Pete Seeger

Education is the big "E" Word. What does education mean? Who do you think educates your children? The teachers at school? Friends? What about discipline? Could it be that children educate themselves through the perception they have of the world around them?

I am sure you have heard, "What a lovely child you have! She/he is so well educated! What a wonderful job you, as parents, have done. She/he puts a napkin in their lap at meals. What pleasant manners your child has." Or perhaps you have heard, "He is such a bad boy! Did you notice that he did not greet us when he arrived? His parents are to be blamed." Or maybe, "Look at that beautiful girl! Did you hear her talking? She speaks just like her mommy. She acts very mature for her age."

I was at a gathering last month, and a mother was there with her three-year-old son. Of course the three-year-old was doing his "job" of running, exploring, not wanting to eat, crying when he was tired, spilling drinks—just doing his marvelous three-year-old job! The mother turned to him and said, "You better start behaving like an adult or Mommy is not going to love you anymore. I am going to tell Daddy that you are not well-educated."

Your children perceive your thoughts and actions. They learn from observation, yet they also create their own reality and their own way to apply the "E" word in their lives.

Have you included in your concept of education the omnipresence of Love? Have you included in your concept of education the intention of kindness? Have you included in your concept of education the demonstration of compassion? What about generosity? What about detachment? I could go on and on and on....Being human is a forever journey. Let's demonstrate with our actions what we want our children to learn from us. Remember the most important demonstration is Love—only Love.

5. SELF-ESTEEM VS. FAKE ESTEEM

o o o o o o o o o o o o o o o o o o o o o o o o o o o o o o

A rich man is one when his pockets are empty,
his children fill his arms.

—Anonymous

Have you seen the thousands of books published to "increase" self-esteem for children, women, men, golfers, lawyers, teachers, and housewives? It is amazing. Doctors speak about self-esteem. Gurus speak about "love yourself." Yoga is promoted as a way to increase self-esteem and personal power. What is real self-esteem? Is it being the best student in the class? Is it being the best dressed? Is it being the one who is always praised on how perfect his or her job was done? Is it being able to count many people as friends and confidants? Is it to have 300 pairs of shoes?

If these things are truly self-esteem, then why are we always looking for more things to fulfill us? More things that can tell us who we are? Things, things, and more things to be acquired? Expecting praise from others in order to feel good or in order to be kind?

For me, the concept of self-esteem used these days is what I have baptized with a new name: fake esteem. True self-esteem cannot be bought by reading a book. True self-esteem cannot come from outside of you. True self-esteem, in my belief, comes from within ourselves, from our own way of thinking, from our own choices and our own perception or sensation of who we truly are.

Be very attentive about your own concept of self-esteem. Remember that low self-esteem is learned at a very young age. Your children are not born with it; they learn it from parents, society and friends. The good thing about this is that anything learned can be unlearned.

Self-esteem is about how we feel about ourselves, not what others think we should do or feel. Self-esteem is the power to remain true to our identity with firm and unshakable roots, no matter what happens in our lives.

To be able to transmit this to your child, you must ask yourself,

What is self-esteem for me?
Who do I think I am?
How do I picture myself?
What is important to me?

Write these questions down and take your time answering them, keeping in mind that when you lift the veils about fake concepts regarding self-esteem, then you will be able to assist your children in building their true concepts, based on awareness, on wisdom, but mostly based on love.

The greatest affirmation to increase self-esteem, both for yourself and for your child is this: I am Love. Say it, repeat it, believe in it, and you will manifest exactly what you affirm to yourself.

6. WHO IS PARENTING YOUR CHILDREN?

o o o o o o o o o o o o o o o o o o o o o o o o o o o o o o o o o o o
Your children need a model of honesty.
If you pretend you have no weaknesses,
and cover them under masks and facades,
your children will learn to do the same
and the game will go on.
Begin today to see and accept
the real you beneath the role.

—*William Martin*
"The Parent's Tao Te Ching"

Who is parenting your children? Is it you, or a role you play? Are you parenting with your own programming, or with your heart? Do your children know you are a human being? Have they seen your tears yet? Do they know that Mommy and Daddy also dream? Have they met the playful you? Do you fear that if you show that which you consider "weakness" your child will not respect you anymore?

As I ask these questions, I contemplate them as well, because if I really ask who is parenting my children, my first response would be Love. Love is parenting my children. I hope you can say the same.

The other night a friend of mine shared with me a beautiful moment she had had with her daughter. She told me that her eight-year-old was crying while in the bathtub. Her grandfather and grandmother had recently died and she was very fond of them. The mother (my friend) heard her crying and said, "Oh honey, it's okay. Don't cry!" The daughter quickly responded, "Mommy, let me cry; don't you see that this is the way sadness disappears?"

So my friend joined her and shared beautiful tears of Love.

I have nothing more to say.

7. JUST TRY—LET GO

○ ○

Children are spiritual beings. They naturally have what many of us spend years trying to reclaim. What if instead of working on "one's inner child" as an adult, we remain in the light of our intrinsic spirituality and retain our childlike wonder and faith? There is a way to do that. If we recognize and honor our children's innate spiritual connection, they may never have to lose it.

—*Mimi Doe and Marsha Walcg, Ph.D.*

Why are we constantly tempted to try to teach, to show, to program our children, either in a practical form or a social or spiritual way? The naturalness and spontaneity of children is *pure* Source and Love. It amazes me how much knowledge grownups are proud of having! Imagine how proud some of us are that our children are behaving just like us—actually "being" us! I have not understood that yet. I do not comprehend when someone comes to me and says, "You are just like your father!" or when they come to my children and say, "Oh, she is just like her grandmother!"

Have you ever just said hello to a child, and truly seen them looking back at you? They are human beings just like you, in a child's body—pure, joyful, unconditionally loving the moment.

For one day, just for one day, I invite you to try not to compare your child with anything or anyone. Try to see how much he/she is unique. Forget about the concept "He is just like his father" or "She is just like her mother." Try to see his/her individuality. Be very attentive, for I believe that to be able to see or to grasp for a single moment the sacred presence of that which your children are, you must be present.

Trust me. If for a single moment you can see with the x-rays of your heart the essence of who your children are, you will have created a very powerful mirror to remind yourself of your uniqueness, your individuality and your own spontaneous and powerful Love.

Just try—let go.

Love is in the air—the air that you and your children breathe.

8. SPEAKING WITH THE HEART

o o o o o o o o o o o o o o o o o o o o o o o o o o o o o o o o
You can speak to your children of life,
but your words are not life itself.
You can show them what you see,
but your showing and your seeing
are forever different things.

Don't mistake your desire to talk
for their readiness to listen.
Far more important are the wordless truths
they learn from you.

—William Martin
"The Parent's Tao Te Ching"

All children deserve to live this life as it is—in love, with fun, and with healthy limits. They deserve to be able to know their immense possibilities as human beings. I know many parents are willing to do whatever is necessary for their children. They read 1001 books about parenting, or about life. They research techniques to become a better parent or how to educate and teach their children to be a better child.

Could you pretend for one moment that words or books do not exist? Pretend that you have none of the programming as to how education should or should not be for you or your children. Imagine that your mind is naked from concepts and imagine your heart has a little mouth speaking to you and guiding you to parent your children in a heartfelt way.

William Martin's words speak to my heart so clearly. It is our joy that transmits joy to our children. It is our willingness to learn from our mistakes that shows our children there are lessons to learn. It is by smelling a flower that we experience the fragrance. How can you explain a flower's fragrance to your child? He must smell the flower for himself. Teaching with the example of living in truth, with love—that is what offers so much more wisdom than any of the concepts or programs we might choose to read about.

When I gave birth to my first child, everyone had something to say to me. My dear friend, Maria Purpura (one of the most loving and courageous mommies I know) told me,

"Many people will tell you a thousand things, but the best advice I can give you is for you to always follow your heart."

With gratitude and joy, I celebrate your child within and all the children in our beautiful world. Please, go smell a flower with your child and remain silent, watching. Feel the fragrance of the flower—for yourself, for your child. Teach with your example, but mostly with grand Love in your heart.

9. BE AWARE

o o o o o o o o o o o o o o o o o o o o o o o o o o o o o o

Tell me, I'll forget.

Show me, I may remember.

But involve me, and I'll understand.

—Chinese Proverb

o o o o o o o o o o o o o o o o o o o o o o o o o o o o o o

Don't worry that children never listen to you.

Worry that they are always watching you.

—Robert Fulghum

Sometimes we, as parents, get so involved with our own worlds, our own perceptions, our own expectations…our own, our own, our own, that I wonder, why do we usually complain when our child begins imitating our behavior, our attitudes, our emotions, and our words—spoken and unspoken?

Two days ago, while I was going to a class, I saw a mother walking with her three-year-old baby. I watched as this child fell and began to cry. Do you know what the mother did? She hit her child and said," Don't do that again!" I was shocked and frozen for a moment. You might be tempted to think, "What a bad mother!" or "That poor child!" If that mother had the knowledge or the *awareness* of being in the moment, of realizing that life with children is a constant surprise, that children sometimes fall, or they usually cry when they are hurt, do you think she would have reacted that way? I felt compassion for that woman, and also for the child. He will learn what he is being unconsciously taught. Be aware that your child is watching. Be aware that your child is feeling. Be aware that your child is present. Be aware that it is your awareness that will guide him to his own awareness, at least for now.

Don't ignore your child because he/she is "just a kid." Enjoy every moment that you are with them. Create a healthy space for you to go to in contemplation every day to recharge your batteries, renew, and create more love with your child. Trust your child, for he is intelligent. Trust your child, for she is wise. Trust your child, for he is pure. Trust your child and invite her to see you how you are, and how you are willing to grow as a parent and as a human being. Trust, invite, love and be aware...*be aware!*

There is no need for you to go to the extreme of thinking, "Oh, I must be quiet. There is my child. I must remain totally silent. He is learning, or watching me so carefully." Just follow your heart; be aware of your words; be mindful of how you treat yourself and how you resolve situations. Watch how *you* are, and from this space of awareness, be aware that your child is indeed learning, absorbing and watching. Mostly, however, be aware that you love your child and that they unconditionally love you.

BE AWARE...

10. PROGRAMMING

o o o o o o o o o o o o o o o o o o o o o o o o o o o o o o o

Skillful speech not only means that we pay attention to the words we speak and to their tone, but also requires that our words reflect compassion and concern for others and that they help and heal, rather than wound and destroy.

—Bhante Henepola Gunaratana

What a tool words are! As Mr. Chick Moorman says, "Words can empower. Words can wound." How aware are you of each word that you say or don't say? How selective are you with the communication skills you have with your children?

In May of 2003 I attended Mr. Alex Slucki's workshop, "The Map of Life." It was a truly enlightening experience for all of us attending because it brought awareness as to how we "grown-ups" are programmed to disrespect children or forget to see the miracle that they are. We are surrounded by things and persons that have programmed us genetically, scientifically, socially and/or spiritually, and then we program others with our own programming. It is a never-ending story! Even though it might be a positive program we are sharing, we are still programming!

One day in the workshop a man told his story. Since he was six years old, his parents always said to him, "You are not a child anymore. Do not behave like a child!" This was repeated to him day after day. Now, he is 35 years old and those child-like, natural qualities of joy, laughter, tears, and delight are buried inside him. He has not allowed them to come to the surface because of the repetition of those words, "You are not a child anymore." He has unconsciously made those untrue words his own. What is most unfortunate is that he has learned to say the same things to his own children.

What I want to share is this: Be aware of your words, and the vibration you put behind them. People have shared with me in my "Personal Power" workshop, "We can't be aware of our words! This is how society speaks. We will sound weird if we consciously select our words!" Well, it is your choice. You know the power of words.

I myself have experienced the power of words, both positively and negatively, both spiritually and socially. Be aware of this when you speak to a child or when you speak to anyone who loves you or trusts you.

Your mind might be engaged in thoughts such as,

"This is good for him/her."
"Severity is what is needed now."
"I will not speak to him/her in this moment."
"My child deserves this."

Please, give yourself a break. We have no time for silly data. We have only this lifetime to love, evolve and grow together—to generate evolution in the most natural way. Choose; be selective…"all-ways" with love!

What are you choosing to think?

What are you choosing to say?

11. THE SOUL OF A CHILD

o o o o o o o o o o o o o o o o o o o o o o o o o o o o o
There are some that still cling to the mistaken conviction
that a child's natural education should be wholly physical;
but the spirit also has its nature, and it is the life of the spirit
that should dominate human existence at every stage.

—*Maria Montessori*

o o o o o o o o o o o o o o o o o o o o o o o o o o o o o o
The secret of all nature is to be found in the soul of a child.

—*Wordsworth*

The more I truly watch my children, the more I want to grow as a parent to be aware of the sacred presence of a child in my life. Here are three separate stories for you to consider.

This weekend I overheard a conversation from a woman talking to a friend. She was saying, "My child will be a grand doctor. His father and I are very proud of him because he is getting the best grades compared to the rest of the children in his classroom. He goes every afternoon to his daddy's office to learn medicine. Sometimes he gets bored, but my husband's discipline teaches him that he has no other option. My son is very well-behaved. He doesn't say a word while we eat, and if he does, I remove his food from the table. Yet I am concerned because his teacher said that he needed more attention and love. She told me he doesn't have any friends! Do you think I should convince the other mothers to fire that silly teacher?"

Then, over the same weekend I saw a well-educated woman who was eight months pregnant. I couldn't contain myself, so I went directly over to hug her and congratulate her. Immediately she said to me, "I am not very happy about being pregnant. This baby was not planned. I don't know what I am going to do with 'it.' My other children drive me crazy already. I just want to kill them. This one, when he comes, he is going to do what I say. This child will have no options!"

Then she abruptly left and went to say "hello" to someone else. I was in shock. I immediately followed her and requested permission to speak to her baby inside her belly. When she said, "Whatever," I bent down and whispered to the child, "Don't take anything personally. You *are* love."

Last Saturday I invited a 17 year-old girl who used to clean our house to visit us. I had heard that she was pregnant and that her husband had abandoned her and mistreated her badly. I sent her a message to come to see me so that I could assist her and offer her some employment. When she arrived, she came over to hug me with her beautiful huge belly and said, "Thank you," with tears in her eyes. She was so full of gratitude that her baby moved each time she hugged me! Of course, my heart melted. Then she told me, "This opportunity that you are giving me, I will not take it for granted. Although I might not have any money or education and I have no one to call for assistance, I have my love that I want to give in its totality to this child!"

There you go. This young woman has no education, no money, yet her spirit is so strong! It was a grand lesson in my own home this weekend—with the added blessing of being able to assist a beautiful, loving and vivacious pregnant woman.

Here you can see that no matter what the appearances are, the most powerful tool, medicine, vitamin, teacher, *everything*, is and will always be Love. Nourish the spirit of your child with love. Fill and feel your child's soul with your heart! It is the best investment you will have ever made in your life!

12. PEELING OFF

o o o o o o o o o o o o o o o o o o o o o o o o o o o o o o o o o
Parenthood is a kind of death.
We're afraid of the death of our individuality,
when it is really our selfishness that dies.
We're afraid of the death of our childlikeness,
when it is really our childishness that dies...
A major initiation of parenthood is this letting go of our false self,
so that our real self can shine forth.

—Joyce and Barry Vissell

What would happen if, at an early age, we were told that our thoughts and personality were wonderful tools to assist us in this "human journey" to create a wonderful experience of life? I imagine that children would remain who they *always* are, instead of growing up to believe that they are their personality and their thoughts! We as parents must be watchful, alert and attentive to this process within ourselves. What are we complaining about? Are we fully enjoying the gift and miracle that parenting is? How can you guide your child without forgetting who he *really* is? When your child is born, you do not care if he has good grades or not. We parents don't care if she is a lawyer or not. We are just so happy and astonished about the miracle of *life!* We are just overwhelmed with the experience of unconditional Love vibrating within a little human being that we can celebrate life with!

Then children grow, along with our mental expectations of them. Of course, certain guidance and healthy limits must be taught. But if you remain true to yourself as a parent, and alert and conscious of what the real important things are, then you will be teaching your child to remain true to themselves.

Who we are is a grand guiding light for our children. I repeat, who *we* are! We are human beings, behind the masks of personality, behaviors, thoughts, feelings, expectations and so on. Our source of love, wisdom and certainty lies within the true self that we are. It is worth the experience of peeling off the layers that blur the vision of the magnificence that parenthood is! Whatever illusion comes off in the peeling, it is a gold mine of new possibilities!

Visualize yourself as often as you can, peeling off anything that you believe might be blurring the way you see your children. While you are peeling off those things, watch and observe the miracle that your child is, and be mindful of your true self in the process. It is worth it.

We have this lifetime to love our children. Why choose not to do so right now?

Job excuses?

Spiritual excuses?

Personal issues?

Whatever…

It is truly a blessing to be able to hug and kiss your child.

I would like to share an inspiring story. John writes, "I grew up in a very poor family. There were days my parents didn't know how they would feed all five of their children. However, they used their ingenuity and we always had something to eat. My parents had faith that God would provide for us. Growing up, I had no idea how poor we were or that our financial situation was so bleak. Thinking back to the days I spent with my parents, brothers and sisters, there was one thing that remained constant: *love*. We were bathed in it every day.

"Because of my parents' ability to love all of us completely and unconditionally, we felt safe. We did many things as a family, together—often searching in the woods for mushrooms that my grandmother would make into soup. I spent hours growing up in the woods, walking with my father. He taught me through his gift of listening to what I had to say and by encouraging me to reach for the stars. He always told his children to stick together, help each other through all our troubles, and rejoice when someone achieved a goal.

"He taught all of us lessons about life: to never give up, to keep on going, to believe in ourselves. He taught us that love is eternal and that money comes and goes. By keeping a constant flow of love, we would always have wealth, because love is the most valuable thing.

"My dad was my first teacher. He set the groundwork for who I am today. My mother taught me the lesson of love through her being. She taught through her example, and she was there to catch all of us when we fell. It was through her pure love that all of us have become outstanding individuals.

"Today I am still very close to all of my family, and I honor my father and my mother for the gift of life and love that they provided. My parents respected their children as individuals and loved the miracle that they created. It's all about *Love* and how we choose to express it."

13. GIVING FROM THE HEART

o o o o o o o o o o o o o o o o o o o o o o o o o o o o o o o

If you want to see what children can do,
you must stop giving them things.

—*N. Douglas*

As conscious, Positive Parents, we try to give our children everything. We try to think of their health, their schooling, give them clothes, toys, vitamins, appropriate food. We give a lot, yes—and it is necessary. Everyone gives from their own possibilities, but the giving is there. But I have noticed that in the giving—from basic necessities to superfluous ones—we sometimes forget about the importance of quality time, of giving something from the heart.

Bestowing a lot of material things or a lot of money on our children sometimes really clutters the possibility of watching the wonders that our children can be, without fancy things. We buy them the newest toy. We want them to dress up like adults! We want them to have many grand possessions, or to have the latest in computers, or to have this, or that. Some parents go to the opposite extreme—no toys, absolutely none!

I have also observed that there is a lot of competition going on in the world of parents. Have you noticed? Have you participated recently in one of these competitions? I overhear, "We traveled to Paris." The response is, "Well, did you know that we went to London?" How about "My child is not like any other child out there. He knows how to behave."

"My child only eats this." "My child only dresses in Gap clothes." Is it really necessary? Do we really need to invest our time in this type of conversation? Do we need to respond to this type of questions with harsh words?

We give education; we give toys; we give money and then we scream it out loud to the world: "See what a good parent we are!" "We know the latest trends in education!" "What a good Daddy he is! He always brings gifts to the children." "What a good Mommy she is! She lets them watch TV whenever they want to."

Having been blessed by the opportunity to be in the presence of orphan children has given me a sense of simplicity and a knock to my head saying things like, "You can give your child the best toys." "You can be the most spiritual parent." "You can offer great teachings to your children." "You can work hard and send them traveling to the most beautiful places on earth." "You can pay for a nanny to take care of your child while you work." "You can bring them gifts when you are away from them." "You can pray for them when you are not with them." "You can manipulate your children with gifts." "You can motivate them to do something by giving them a toy, or a puppy." Yet you will never know what exactly they are thinking, what they are feeling and sensing from all of these things.

Is your child's happiness created by receiving a toy, or is it created by the one who delivers it? The giving, when it is expressed with joy and love, turns the tiniest toy into the biggest one, the most simple dress into a princess gown, a little play car into something grand and wonderful to play with. I could go on and on. Everything is a *choice—your choice!* Whatever you think you are giving, ask yourself *why?* Whatever your excuses, ask yourself *why?*

Children do not need to be overwhelmed with things, concepts, spiritual training, and so on. Children are love. They give love and they need love. The orphans I have worked with have taught me a great lesson. They delight so much in a smile returned that they dream and they imagine more fulfilling possibilities with love. They, like all positive children, are content with the simplest things.

Give a hug to your children. Be grateful that they are alive. Whatever you give to them as possessions, education, and so on—give it consciously and lovingly in a celebratory way, while always setting healthy limits for your child and yourself. Just remember what it was like when you were a child. Do you now remember how many toys you had—or do you remember how much or how little time your parents were with you? I mean, really *with* you?

14. SHARING: A NATURAL PROCESS

o o o o o o o o o o o o o o o o o o o o o o o o o o o o o o o
When we make a child "share," it is not sharing.

—*Magda Gerber*

o o o o o o o o o o o o o o o o o o o o o o o o o o o o o o o
Observe more, do less.

—*Magda Gerber*

"You need to be a good girl, a good boy. You *must* share your toys with your friends. Be nice; don't be rude. Good children share." Have you heard these words before? Have you applied them to yourself? Why do we want to *force* sharing? Is it really for the children to learn "sharing," or for us as parents to give a good impression to other parents or with our own mind's programming?

What if we applied the concept of sharing to grownups? Let me offer some examples:

"David, be a good man, share all your money with your friends. You are a good man, aren't you?"

"Caroline, be nice. Share your husband with others. Do not behave like the jealous wife; be nice and share."

"Veronica, I want you to give me your car because I don't have one. Share it with me; don't be rude!"

Why on earth would something as natural as *sharing* need to be coerced and imposed by us "grownups" to the natural ebb and flow that children are? Are we truly grownups? Do we really understand what growing up means?

I have noticed that when both children and adults are *not* told things like "You must share." "You must say you love me." "You must give mommy a kiss." "You must come home from work early." "You must not speak with her." "You must invite them over." "You must not play like that," then they naturally decide to share and love because a space of freedom and choice arises. The element of control becomes a limitation for the natural flowering of the human experience of sharing. All this does not only apply to the concept of sharing; it applies to love as well.

"Daniel (who is six-years-old), go kiss your uncle and be a nice boy." (This is the first time that Daniel has ever met this uncle.)

"Rebecca, don't you want to give a hug to your mommy's friend? Go give her a hug right now." Meanwhile, Rebecca has perceived something that she doesn't like about her mommy's friend and is reticent to come close.

"Alex, tell my friend that you love her, and hurry up because we are leaving now." (Alex's mommy wants Alex to say "I love you" to a friend of hers so she won't feel embarrassed.)

Did you know that coercing and forcing this natural expression of love has increased the percentage of children who are abused on our planet?

Please, do not decide to go to the extreme and think, "Well, if I don't tell my children to share, they will always be rude." You might think that if children are physically hurting each other, to decide not to interfere would be detrimental because they don't want to share. Be very conscious. Give a space to your children for growth, while setting healthy limits for them.

If I give you a cutting from the most precious orchid in the world, would you keep it without planting it because of "its uniqueness" or your fear of losing it? Of course not! You would plant it in the most perfect place, with the right mixture of earth, the right humidity, the right space for the orchid to grow, and you would look forward to being able to watch that most rare and unique flower blossom.

Let your children grow, too. Observe them, set healthy limits, and allow those natural expressions of love (like sharing and kissing) to blossom naturally so they can flow from the heart and not from the programming that they *must* share in order to please Mommy and Daddy but not be true to themselves.

Think about the consequences.

15. TRANSMITTING CONSCIOUSNESS

o o o o o o o o o o o o o o o o o o o o o o o o o o o o o o o o

No printed word, nor spoken plea
Can teach young minds what men should be.
Not all the books on all the shelves—
But what the teachers are themselves.

—Anonymous

o o o o o o o o o o o o o o o o o o o o o o o o o o o o o o o o

The condition of our consciousness registers directly in the child's consciousness, and it is accordingly translated into well-being or distress.

—Polly Brendel

o o o o o o o o o o o o o o o o o o o o o o o o o o o o o o o o

It is well known that 95% of a child's learning process goes on automatically through unconscious imprinting to the models available. Studies have reported that only 5% of the young child's mind is available to us for conscious "manipulation" through verbal training. All our demands, instructions, and orders to modify the child's behavior address only 5% of his learning process, and our unexpressed thoughts and feelings teach his other 95%—below the level of consciousness.

—Joseph Chilton Pearce

I have noticed that whenever I create myself as unbalanced, or tired, or "stressed," that is when my children sleep less, are more cranky or call my attention to ways that "a parent's mind" might judge as non-appropriate. I have become more aware of this connection between my children's moods and my moods, and now each time that I perceive my children as "unbalanced," I go within and check out what is going on with my process: How do I feel? Am I being present in the moment? Am I giving quality time to my children? Am I physically with them, but is my mind somewhere else?

As soon as I regain awareness of the transmission of my emotions to them, immediately—like magic—balance and harmony manifest again. Be aware of your spoken and unspoken teachings to your beautiful children.

Meditation, physical activity, positive thinking, using a diary, singing, dancing, arranging for some quiet time—these are just a few of the tools available to assist us in having a clear mind so we are able to guide our children through the grandest wisdom ever—which is the power of our Love. Let us tap into the Love that we all are and have empathy toward our children's moods and feelings, and mostly with our own. Let us remember constantly that moods are like clouds that come and go. Moods are like the weather—unpredictable sometimes. What remains is the awareness that Love is the Power that reminds us of what is important. Remember that the more you love, the more you create love. Begin with yourself and the rest (your children) will follow.

16. IMAGINATION

o o o o o o o o o o o o o o o o o o o o o o o o o o o o o o o o o

Imagination is more important than knowledge.

—Albert Einstein

o o o o o o o o o o o o o o o o o o o o o o o o o o o o o o o o o

Who knows the thoughts of a child?

—Nora Perry

Have you ever wondered what your child is thinking about? Have you ever really observed your child when he/she is playing with his/her imagination? Are you aware of the miracle happening when your child is thinking and playing?

I overheard a conversation the other day as a father was yelling at his eleven-year-old son who was imagining that a plastic cup he was holding was a space-ship. "Imagination is stupid," the father said. "You had better focus on the important things of life if you don't want to end up a loser." The child, with tears in his eyes, asked, "What is a loser? You are always saying that I should be like you, Daddy. If imagination is stupid, why are you always telling Mom that your dream car is a red one? Are you a loser, Daddy?"

Wow! I was truly impressed at the boy's honesty. Whoever stops imagining? Whoever stops dreaming? Maybe some people think that dreaming or imagination is stupid, or that it is only for children. Examine the truth inside yourself. Don't you have dreams? Don't you use your imagination? If you do, how do you use it? Is it for positive or for negative thinking?

We don't know what our children are thinking. We don't know when a little piece of paper will be transformed into a grand palace with some crayons. We don't know when a balloon will be transformed into an imaginary planet. The only thing we can do is to imagine the power and the purity that our children are and to offer them a safe place to express that.

Imagine the power of love, and like John Lennon sang,

Imagine…

17. THREE POWERFUL WORDS

o o o o o o o o o o o o o o o o o o o o o o o o o o o o o o o o o
Love is what makes you smile when you're tired.

—Terri, four years old

o o o o o o o o o o o o o o o o o o o o o o o o o o o o o o o o o
If you want to learn to love better,
you should start with a friend that you hate.

—Nikka, six years old

o o o o o o o o o o o o o o o o o o o o o o o o o o o o o o o o o
There are two kinds of love: our love,
God's love. But God makes both kinds.

—Jenny, four years old

o o o o o o o o o o o o o o o o o o o o o o o o o o o o o o o o o
You really shouldn't say "I love you" unless you mean it. But if
you mean it, you should say it a lot. People forget.

—Jessica, eight-years old

There were 150 people who attended the interactive workshop, "The Parent Talk Experience," given by Mr. Chick Moorman and Dr. Thomas Haller. During the three-day intensive sessions, we learned and practiced various aspects of parenting: The Language of Personal Power, Anger Management, Parent Talk, Words that Empower And Words that Wound, Spirit Whisperers (teachers who nourish a child's spirit) and Couple Talk.

It was an incredible, enlightening opportunity for us all. We were gifted with many useful tools for our Parenting Toolbox, and we practiced new skills to improve our family interactions, to enrich the quality of our thoughts and our choice of words with our children, with our partners, and with ourselves. Yet, what impressed me most was that all the teachings and wisdom we received can be summed up in one word: LOVE.

There is no greater power; there is no greater tool; there is no greater transmission than the transmission of love. It was from the pure space of love that Mr. Moorman and Dr. Haller shared their wisdom with us. It was with grand hope that the audience received their sharing. I really recommend this experience for all of you in the journey of parenting, teaching and being human.

Maybe you cannot attend workshops. Perhaps you cannot read any parenting books. What if you are busy with your business, or you don't have extra money for things like that? Maybe you wonder and you think: I would love to learn more about parenting. I would like to be a more conscious parent. I want my children to be happy. I want them to grow, free from manipulations and coercive behaviors. I want them to never forget who they are. If this is the way you think, let me tell you something. You already have the most important thing inside you that will accompany your children all through their lives—that is who you really are, the love that you feel, the love that you manifest yourself to be, as kindness, patience and respect.

Start by saying I LOVE YOU…Love feeds itself with love and generates more love with the expression of love. Say it, live it, transmit it to your children. Tell your children, I love you. Realize that it is in this moment that you are alive. In this moment you are breathing. In this moment you have a choice to say I love you or not.

I LOVE YOU.

18. WHOM DO YOU CHOOSE TO BE?

o o o o o o o o o o o o o o o o o o o o o o o o o o o o o o o
It is good to control your words and thoughts.
The seeker who is in control feels free and joyful.
Listen to that seeker who guards his tongue and speaks wisely.
Such a one is humble and does not exalt himself.

—*"The Dhammapada"*

Helen awoke upset and angry. She had experienced a hard week, with lots of work to do, four children to attend to, and she was not very motivated for another "ordinary day." She began rushing her children to get ready for school, preparing their lunches and breakfasts—all the multiple tasks that she needed to accomplish everyday before leaving the house. Helen began to feel desperate when her three-year old, Eileen pulled her skirt to get her attention. She pushed her daughter away and said, *"DON'T BOTHER ME NOW!"* Immediately Eileen started crying and began to wail, "Mommy? Mommmyyyyy? Where are you?" Helen knelt down and said, "I am right here, honey." Her daughter continued screaming, "Mommy? Mommy? Where are you?" Helen, frightened now, responded in a louder tone of voice, *"I AM RIGHT HERE!"* The child was silent for a moment and then she went over to her mother, her face lined with deep concern and astonishment. She told her to open her mouth and Eileen whispered, "Don't worry, Mommy. I will give kisses to the grumpy monster so that it will disappear and you can come out!" Of course, what followed were tears from Helen and kisses from Eileen.

Who are we creating ourselves to be? What role or disguise are we wearing? If your life was a movie (maybe it is) what part would you like to play in it? An extra? An actor? A director or producer? Whatever the role you play, how are you choosing to create yourself? Are you disguised as the grumpy father? Are you disguised as the busy mommy? Are you disguised as the tired soldier? Are you disguised as part of the ruling class? Are you disguised as a spiritual teacher? Whatever the disguise or costume you choose to wear in your movie, are you aware that beyond the costume your presence is what animates the disguise?

Remember that your children are watching you. The more they watch the same habit of yours, or the same disguise or mask, the more they will integrate it into their reality. Just like when a child watches a movie over and over again, they become Peter Pan, or Cinderella, or Captain Hook, or The Wicked Witch.

What role are you playing? What are your children learning from you? Who are you choosing to be? Do you want to try an experiment? For one week, pretend that you will disguise yourself as Love. Every morning when you wake up, put on your Love costume. Wear it, believe in it, create your movie being Love. In the process, watch the response of your children. Choose to create the movie of Love along with them.

19. VULNERABILITY EQUALS STRENGTH

o o o o o o o o o o o o o o o o o o o o o o o o o o o o o o o
Out of your vulnerabilities will come your strength.

—Sigmund Freud

o o o o o o o o o o o o o o o o o o o o o o o o o o o o o o o
A mother, even at the risk of her own life, protects her child, her only child.

In the same way, you should cultivate love without measure toward all beings.

You should cultivate toward the whole world—above, below, around—a heart of love unstinted, unmixed with any sense of differing or opposing interests.

You should maintain this mindfulness all the time you are awake.

Such a state of heart is the best in the world.

—Majjhima Nikaya

Sometimes we, as parents, judge ourselves harshly for the mistakes we make with our beloved children. We think about how we could have acted differently in certain moments. I was speaking to a friend who told me, "I have so many weaknesses. I try and try but I repeat the same habits over and over again! When I am tired, I scream at my children! Sometimes I have been physically violent toward them. I feel like I am the worst mother in the world. At 5:00 p.m., always at that exact time, I feel so exhausted! I can't stand to hear any more noise. My children seem to choose exactly that moment to fight and scream at each other! Oh, what am I to do?"

If we know our vulnerabilities and our weaknesses, we are blessed! Then we have the opportunity to sort them out, to source them and to do something about them! If we know that exactly at 5:00 we become overwhelmed, then at 4:30 we need to arrange a time to meditate, or put some soothing music on, or simply be aware that exactly at 5:00 the things that we don't like might happen! It is very simple. The things we complain about, I believe, are the things that we could use as great tools to empower ourselves, to increase our personal power, to detach more from our expectations and start living and loving in the now.

Remember that we are always at choice. Know that is okay to make mistakes. Mistakes are opportunities to learn how to *DO IT* more consciously the next time or how *NOT* to fall into the same habit patterns. It is okay to feel tired. It is okay to feel whatever we choose to feel. Never forget, however, that whatever your experience is, *YOU ALWAYS HAVE A CHOICE* about how to create that moment and who you choose to be.

Do not be afraid to be vulnerable. Power does not come by saying, "I never make mistakes," or "My children should see who is in command." Real power emerges from Love. Real power emanates from the power to forgive. Real power offers the possibility to keep on moving. Real power supports us to want to learn and evolve and to recognize the joy of being a parent; and the opportunity to see what we need to work on inside ourselves. The true power for any parent, for any human being comes from Love...towards oneself and the rest of the world. Source your mistakes with Love. Love is a choice, your choice. Will you take it, or not? Remember that whatever you choose to be, your children are watching and learning.

20. CHOICE OF WORDS

o o o o o o o o o o o o o o o o o o o o o o o o o o o o o o o
Our words are like seeds we plant in our minds.

They take root and sprout. If repeated often enough, words grow into attitudes and beliefs. Never doubt the power of words—whether self talk or talk we have accepted from others.

—Peggy Jenkins, Ph.D.

It is said that, "In the beginning was the Word." We need to be aware that words are something we must be attentive to—especially the words we choose to say to ourselves and to our beloved children. I myself have used words that I wish I had not said to my children—words that take more time to heal or to be transformed into a positive mood than the time it took for me to say them.

I know some people that say that words are not important, that their children do not understand them, or that their children need harsh words because they deserve it. I want to invite you to go inside yourself right now and ask yourself these questions:

Are there any words that you would have wished your parents had not said to you?

Are there any words you would have wished you did not say to someone you love?

Are there any words that carry anger when you express them?

What do you think others feel when they hear those words?

Are you aware that words are the basic, most important tool for hypno-therapists?

Are you aware that a child's brain development has an enormous impact on the words they hear both when they are in the womb and out of it?

What are the feelings that arise in you with these contemplations?

What words would you choose to say right now to your child?

For one week, I invite you to choose your words carefully. You can do it! It is a choice, as always. Your children deserve it. They will learn from the choice of words you select, and most probably they will repeat them. Teach them to choose their words, through compassion, healthy limits and as always and through *LOVE*.

21. CELEBRATING LIFE

o o o o o o o o o o o o o o o o o o o o o o o o o o o o o o o

I give thanks for this joyous day:
Miracle shall follow miracle
and joy never cease.

—Peggy Jenkins

o o o o o o o o o o o o o o o o o o o o o o o o o o o o o o o

Smile with me and spread the cheer
Radiate from here and here.

—Peggy Jenkins

What can be more beautiful than children laughing? What can be more beautiful that children smiling at you? What can be more beautiful than little hands communicating with their touch that they love you? What can be more beautiful than to hear our children breathing peacefully? What can be more beautiful than to be hugged by your child? What can be more beautiful than nurturing your child's tears? What can be more beautiful than being alive?

Focus yourself and your children on the positive. Focus on the good that exists in the world. Focus on the beauty that nature is. Focus on the joy of being alive. Focus on the blessing of living with an open heart!

Celebrate Life! Celebrate the Positive Child!

22. HUMAN BEING VS. HUMAN DOING

o o o o o o o o o o o o o o o o o o o o o o o o o o o o o o

Some parents convey to their child that she-he is worthy of love only if she-he lives up to her parents' expectations and is successful.

This conditional Love creates a child who is a human doing, in which how she-he feels about herself is overly connected with her-his accomplishments.

—Jim Taylor, Ph.D.

How much some of us confuse Being with Doing! This does not apply only to professional lawyers, teachers, administrators or doctors. This also applies to those of us who are parents. Are we demanding that our children be the best in school? Are we bragging about our children's accomplishments? Are we focusing on what our children are DOING rather than who our children ARE?

What are your expectations for your child?

Do you expect him to be a grand doctor?

Do you expect him to be a lawyer?

Do you expect him to be a writer?

Do you expect him to be the next Dalai Lama?

Do you expect him to save the world?

Some of you must be thinking, I just want my child to be happy. Be aware, that this phrase too, is an expectation. I believe, with all my heart that who your child is, is happiness itself. Who your child is, is beauty itself. Who your child is, is creation itself!

What expectations did you try to fulfill for your parents?

What expectations did you not "accomplish"?

Do you feel guilty about it?

Do you feel proud of yourself because you are now the lawyer that everyone was expecting?

The dancer that everyone praises?

The perfectly gorgeous woman seen on magazine covers?

Now let me ask you: Do you want your children to feel that way, too?

Do you want your children to live their lives just to make YOU happy?

To make you proud?

To be liked by others?
Are you living your life that way?

DO YOU KNOW WHO YOUR CHILDREN ARE?
CAN YOU EVER, REALLY KNOW?
We must begin with knowing ourselves!

23. CHOICES, ANYONE?

o o o o o o o o o o o o o o o o o o o o o o o o o o o o o o o o

It is not our abilities that show what we truly are.
It is our choices.

—Professor Dumbledore to Harry in
"Harry Potter and the Chamber of Secrets," by J.K. Rowling

I've been traveling for almost a month now and I have had the opportunity to meet many beautiful new friends that are also on the journey of conscious parenting. They are human beings just like all of us, in the journey of *CHOICES*. I keep on repeating this word, *CHOICES* in these pages. It serves as a reminder to me, and I believe it has a *HUGE* impact on how we parent, how we love, how we guide, and how we treat ourselves!

Could we increase the possibilities for our children to choose more positive things in their lives if we, ourselves, *PRACTICE* the power of choice? What if we decide, as parents, not only to read books about parenting, but to dutifully follow instructions for educating our children, disciplining them, feeding them, reading to them and so on? If, before applying these tools to our children, we first considered what we are doing in our lives and began to ask ourselves:

Do I really believe in choices?

Do I really want my child to be the positive being he already is?

Am I positive myself?

Do I demand from my children to *BE POSITIVE* while I scream at my employees and do not show respect to my friends?

Do I speak about doing positive things in the world but the first chance I have I judge and criticize how negative others are being?

I met wonderful beings that are parenting their children with all their hearts—with complete trust in love—and they are looking to evolve and become better parents in all ways possible. However, we must apply that *CHOICE* in ourselves!

How can we parents become more positive? There are many ways, tools, techniques: meditation, prayer, affirmations, observing nature, listening to classical music, reading positive books, gathering with friends that support the same ideas—there are many possibilities! It is about what you choose to do. No one can choose your way for you.

This is the moment to Love.
This is a positive intention.
The *YOU* who reads this is *THE POSITIVE YOU.*

24. SKILLS

o o o o o o o o o o o o o o o o o o o o o o o o o o o o o o o o
Say one word with your mouth shut!

—Zen saying

o o o o o o o o o o o o o o o o o o o o o o o o o o o o o o o o
The more you know, the less you understand.

—Tao Te Ching

What an amazing journey it is being a parent. There are so many possibilities! So many possible choices! So many thoughts and emotions! The other day a friend told me, "Applying skillfully learned skills with love transforms the skills to tools. Applying skills without love transforms the skills into burdens and limitations. Not being concerned about skills, enjoying the moment—hugging a child—expands as Love and no skills are needed."

I contemplated this for a long time. *SKILLS, SKILLS, AND SKILLS*. Then I began noticing how many people talk about skills, how many people praise skills and focus on skills sometimes without even being aware that they are doing that.

I noticed a father saying, "My son is very skillful. He can paint and play the piano. I love him for that." Another mother commented about her daughter, "She is involved in piano lessons, cooking lessons, ballet and swimming lessons. She can do a lot of things!" Another mother was saying, "My technique for parenting is the ONLY one that works. I don't understand why there are parents that do not learn the skills of this system! They are so unconscious if they don't do it my way—the way that this technique and system says it must be done."

Of course, having skills are good, but are they all we need as parents or as human beings? I would like to invite you to pretend that you have not learned anything about parenting. You must include what you have learned in your own mind, and through your own parents and surroundings.

Contemplate this: If there were no books to read, if judgments did not existed, and you were aware that this is your *ONLY* moment to *LOVE YOUR CHILD*, how would you guide him? How much quality time would you share with her? Would you demand from other parents not to make mistakes with their child? Would you demand from others to learn your skills? Would you demand from your child to do, do, and do—to continue to learn more and more skills? Or would you, along with your child, learn together, create together, hold hands in the growth process until your child is ready to walk in life with his own tools?

For one week I invite you to pretend that the only skill you do, feel and create perfectly well—the only skill that you have learned and you will need to learn—is *LOVE*. Just pretend like a child. What would you do differently now? Would you say I *LOVE YOU* more? Would you drop any judgment or expectation regarding your family, children and loved ones? Would you have the courage to contact a loved one that your mind has decided not to talk to anymore?

Just pretend. Observe yourself, then observe your child.

To close, I'll leave you with these words from my daughter, Alhia, who is five years old: "Mommy, why do you and your friends give workshops? Why are you always trying to learn more about how to be good parents? You all do so much! You all get tired! You all get upset! You all forget to relax! This is just a game! I love you."

25. SILENCE

o o o o o o o o o o o o o o o o o o o o o o o o o o o o o o o o o
These people honor me with their lips, but their heart is far from
me;
In vain do they worship me, teaching as doctrines the precepts of
men.

—The Gospel of Matthew 15:4-9

o o o o o o o o o o o o o o o o o o o o o o o o o o o o o o o o o
In the beginner's mind there are many possibilities,
but in the expert's mind there are few.

—Shunryu Suzuki, Roshi

Beloved friends, we here in Cancun, all of the volunteers of Mastery Life have decided to focus on fifteen days of silence. We have chosen only to express through writing our needs and requests, and it has been a most interesting thing to watch these last few days. Obviously, considering that some of us are in the Mastery Journey of Parenthood with young children who do not read yet, instead of silence, using as few words as possible is challenging sometimes, but MOSTLY very rewarding.

I, for example, have a very talkative personality. So, this has been an extremely challenging experience for me. At the same time, we all have found something special that words cannot convey. It has been such a rewarding experience that we have decided to continue this focus for an additional fifteen days. Doing our best to use the minimum of words (without ceasing to be spontaneous, of course) we contemplate the necessity of speaking before we do so. (My husband is very happy with this new me!)

There is a saying of Sai Baba's that goes like this: "Speak only if it improves silence." We want to invite you to create this "silent energy field" for the next week or two. It is also suggested that you journal about your experiences especially about what you observe differently about yourself in silence. You can focus those moments you want to speak out the most. When is the moment you wish not to speak at all?

Many teachings say, *BE SILENT. QUIET YOUR MIND. MEDITATE.* This is great and wonderful, especially if you live on an ashram or away from the world. What if your Journey of Mastery is manifesting in the corporate world, or as a doctor assisting and healing others[1]? As a schoolteacher being blessed to guide others in learning? As a father or mother having one or more children, trying to do your best to guide them while keeping your sanity?

Well, let's create a practical exercise. We at Mastery Life practice "Fasting from Words." Many people fast with fruit, juices, water, or raw foods. Let's do a fast from speaking. Again, please don't go to extremes, however. Only for a week or two let your focus be *THE PRACTICE OF SILENCE.*

Vicki Falcone writes about the "Soul Process" in her book, *Buddha Never Raised Kids and Jesus Didn't Drive Carpool: Seven Principles for Parenting with Soul* from Jodere Publishers. It is a good reminder for us and I recommend that you read it. Here is a bumper sticker created and included in Mrs. Falcone's book to assist you during this time of "Word Fasting."

> S=SILENCE
> O=OBSERVE
> U=UNDERSTAND
> L=LISTEN

I think we can do it and experience it…What about you?
Shhhh.

---

1.   The August 2003 issue of *Canadian Medical Association Journal* reports that an optimistic attitude can do wonders for patients' recovery. The research reviewed sixteen studies that spanned 30 years. Reporting for ABC News, Medical Correspondent Dr. Nancy Snyderman on *Good Morning America* said, "This mind-body connection that we have been toying with for the past couple of decades really does have hard science behind it." (See: http://abcnews.go.com/sections/living/Healthywoman/positive010723.html)

26. STAYING AWAKE AS A POSITIVE PARENT

o o o o o o o o o o o o o o o o o o o o o o o o o o o o o

Therefore, Ananda, do not be the judge of people;

do not make assumptions about others.

A person is destroyed by holding judgments about others.

—Anguttura Nikaya

o o o o o o o o o o o o o o o o o o o o o o o o o o o o o

The Buddha said: "This most subtle awakening comes about through moment-to-moment attentiveness. By way of attentiveness, there is attunement to the ways in which things manifest, such as form and consciousness. The practitioner awakens to perfect wisdom by becoming blissfully free from obsessions with habits, names, sense experiences, personal feelings, and with dread of dying and all the despair that goes with it."

—"The Dhammapada"

As I was waiting for Mrs. Inspiration to come through me to write, suddenly a thought appeared in my mind. *THE POSITIVE CHILD.* Our children deserve the best of all we as parents can be, but what about us, as parents? Why do we rate other parents with our own expectations, judgments, and comparisons? Why is it that we condemn or praise other parents only by the way we think they should be?

When the "Positive Child Way of Living" manifested for the first time a couple of years ago, I asked my meditation teacher about it. He told me, 'It is a wonderful idea—working with children, giving them positive tools—but first the parent needs to realize *The Positive Child within himself!* If not, there will be a moment when something is not going to make sense."

As my awareness began contemplating this memory, I began to listen more and more to phrases spoken every day by many people (including myself). Over the last three days I have heard phrases like:

"Oh, you are a great mother because you rarely sleep!"

"He is a great father! He changes the baby's diapers at night!"

"Oh, what a good Mom—she stays with her children the whole day!"

"What a good Dad he is. He never misses any of his son's football games."

"What a good Mom. She gives all her time to her children!"

"Oh, he is such a good Dad. He never goes out with his colleagues. He is a family man!"

"Look at that mother with her kids! She is so grumpy! She probably is not a very good mother."

"I heard Adriana's husband never goes to any of the children's festivals. He is always too busy!"

"Look how awful that lady looks! She should take better care of herself rather than giving all of her time to her kids."

"Look how much time that mother spend in the salon! She should spend more time with her children."

I also hear other phrases that people involved on the "spiritual path" use regularly, like: "She is such a good mother. She teaches meditation techniques to her children."

"He is a good Dad. He is never late from work, so he can speak about religion to his family during dinner every night."

"What a conscious family they are! They eat perfectly balanced meals and never watch TV!"

"What an unconscious family they are. The kids are always screaming. They probably watch television all day long."

I could go on, and on, and on. Can you see that all of these phrases, although some seem positive and others seem negative—even if they WERE based on truthful facts—are our perceptions, our interpretations and our judgments?

What if your judgment regarding someone as being a good mother or a good father is mistaken? Have you ever considered thinking, "I wonder what their life is like?" Or "I wonder what experiences she or he has had?"

Now, *BE ATTENTIVE*. I don't want to encourage the "So What?" behavior. I'm not advocating the "This is how I am and I am not going to change!" mindset. Neither do I want to encourage the "Everything happens for a reason attitude," which may or may not include emotional child abuse, physical violence towards children, harsh words, and so on. These would be indicators of the kind of behavior that signals unconsciousness, imbalance and a tremendous need for assistance! This is not the way for *THE POSITIVE CHILD AND THE POSITIVE PARENT!*

I want to invite you to allow yourself to learn, to continue the wonderful job you are doing as a parent, to keep focused on the positive feelings, emotions, and dreams that reside inside your heart and soul! I encourage you to use your energy to see the positive in everything—starting with you!

Please don't be disappointed in what others think about you. Please don't strive to be the best father or mother you can be by doing exactly what society, family, friends and non-friends expect you to do!

Remember: *YOU HAVE A CHOICE! FOLLOW YOUR HEART!*

Use your common sense, and as the Mayans say: "TIAHUITL," which means "GO! CONTINUE! ADELANTE!"

Stay awake!

You are a positive parent-child yourself!

Now let me share a letter from one of the Mastery of Life members who is reminding us of the power of choice:

Dear Ivonne,

Please feel free to share my story. It was wonderful to meet you and your beautiful children. What a blessing I received! Your book, *The Soulmate Called God* had a strong impact on me, yet left me with a very peaceful experience. That allowed me to share this part of my life with you.

I am 67 years old. I once was married, twenty years ago, to a beautiful woman, Margaret, fifteen years younger than I. We had two beautiful sons (twins) and we had a wonderful family. After my sons were born, I began to be obsessed with my discoveries regarding alternative medicine and possible natural solutions for cancer. I was so obsessed with my belief that I could create an impact in the medical world and assist many people, I lost sight of what was there at hand for me—my children and my dear Soulmate.

My wife tried many times to tell me, "We are here. Your children need you." I just thought they were not understanding my work! I thought that they were very egotistic in not seeing that I was about to *CHANGE THE WORLD!* Of course, I became so obsessed my wife finally left me and I decided not to contact her or my children again, until I could come back to them with the proof in my hands of my belief. Years passed by, exactly thirteen years, in which I created a successful Health Center in Germany. Many people were cured from many illnesses, mainly cancer in the early stages.

In my life, I have always meditated and have believed that everything was just as it is. I believed that God wanted things as they were, until one day, a feeling struck me and a voice without words whispered in my heart, "Yes, everything is just as it is, because YOU create it that way." In that moment, my ego dropped to my knees; tears came out from my soul and eyes and I decided to pack my bags and look for my wife and children. I knew they were living in a town just two hours away. I drove there, arrived at my mother-in-laws house and just when I was about to tell her how sorry I was, she said, "Shhhh, it is over. Margaret and the boys died in a car accident a week ago."

That moment stopped my whole existence. I couldn't cry anymore, nor could I honestly feel guilty about it. All I felt was the great responsibility of the consequences of my choices. Of course, I dreamed of hugging them, kissing them, and being with them. Yet, that day I knew that God truly lives inside us. We *CO-CREATE* our realities, as you usually say. We are responsible for them.

Please, take this sharing as just a sharing, but if I could give all of you advice, it would be, don't miss any opportunity you have to hug your children, to tell them how much you love them! The greatest gift is to love! Don't take your loved ones for granted, and if you have found a Soulmate, like I did once, don't be afraid of that relationship. Go for it. The rest is the background in the big theater of life.

Sincerely,
Walter G., Germany

PART VII
POSITIVE RESOURCES

o o o o o o o o o o o o o o o o o o o o o o o o o o o o o o o o

When you are deluded and full of doubt,
even a thousand books of scripture are not enough.
When you have realized understanding,
even one word is too much.

—*Fen Yang*

PART VII
POSITIVE RESOURCES

In my journey as a parent, I have never stopped wanting to learn the positive tools and unlearn the negative tools that will assist me in becoming a better human being. I want to do my best in the magical and enormous responsibility of guiding and raising children consciously, while guarding and respecting their individuality and uniqueness at all times. To aid this intention of mine, I have found wonderful contributors in the world that are creating an impact, not only in the education of children, but in the protection of the child as a spiritually conscious being.

There are already many resources and books that will give you not one, but hundreds of suggestions. When I see too many suggestions, however, I become overwhelmed and sometimes confused as to what to choose or not to choose. I also see that there are so many choices that often the full schedule of a parent allows us only to create the space to relax for a moment, read a few paragraphs and then it's time for bed!

This next section offers a few suggestions that have been extremely useful in my own experience. I have seen an immediate transformation not only in my children but for myself as well.

Remember, as with all information shared in *The Positive Child*, I suggest you follow your heart. See what fits best with your own ideas and emotions, and remember these are only tools for the beautiful journey of parenthood. Never forget that the most important teacher, assistant and tool you will ever find to guide you in raising your children positively and consciously is the Power of Love residing in your own heart. I hope I can be of service to you in any way possible through my own experience.

Also, remember that the best education, the most wonderful toys or the most famous parenting books can never empower your children the way you can through the *modeling* of your *Positive Thinking*, through the *Power of Affirmations* and through the *Language of Love*.

POSITIVE WEBSITES

RIE method: www.rie.org
Parent Talk System: www.chickmoorman.com
Montessori Educational System: www.montessori.org
The Conscious Family: www.susankramer.com
Growing Healthy Kids: www.growinghealthykids.com
Peace on Earth: www.WeWantPeaceOnEarth.com
Children of The New Earth www.childrenofthenewearth.com

BABY SONGS www.babysongs.com
Songs for Peace: http://www.songs4peace.com/
Hap Palmer www.happalmer.com
Mozart Effect: www.mozarteffect.com

POSITIVE BOOKS

The 10 commitments, Parenting with Purpose
By Chick Moorman and Thomas Haller
A must for all parents even before giving birth to a child. So far one of the best and most simple books I've ever read. This book should be in the hands and hearts of educators, nurses, doctors, parents and all those who are blessed to be close to any child. It is a message that will transcend time, belief, and space.

The Parent's Tao Te Ching: Ancient Advice for Modern Parents
By William C. Martin
This book is a great place for parents to begin their study since it captures the essence of raising a child.

Spirit Whisperers: Teachers Who Nourish a Child's Spirit
By Chick Moorman
This is an inspirational and practical guide for teaching from the heart—truly a MUST for any parent and educator. The genius heart of Mr. Chick Moorman created a masterpiece of love by writing this book. Find out if you are a Spirit Whisperer or not.

The Parent Talk System: How to Talk to Your Children in Language That Builds Self-Esteem and Encourages Responsibility
By Chick Moorman

This language system based on personal power, assists both parent and child without programming to be responsible and respectful toward oneself and one another. Personally, it has helped my whole family enrich the tools that words are!

Meditations for Mothers of Toddlers
By Beth Wilson Saavedra
Uplifting to read, this is a nice reminder for exhausted mothers and anyone that needs a little pat on the back from time to time.

Dear Parent: Caring for Infants with Respect
By Magda Gerber
Great tools for new parents, especially for children from 0-3 years of age.

Discovery of the Child
By Maria Montessori
A true discovery of your own inner child that will reflect on your children.

Couple Talk: How to Talk Your Way to a Great Relationship
By Chick Moorman and Thomas Haller
How to treat your partner with respect because your children are always watching. Ninety-five percent of what your children learn is through pure observation, so please be aware, parents, of your words and actions.

The Joyful Child: A Sourcebook of Activities and Ideas for Releasing Children's Natural Joy
By Peggy Davison Jenkins, Ph.D.
This book is not just for the children in your life. It is also for you, dear parents.

Curriculum of Love: Cultivating the Spiritual Nature of Children
By Morgan Simone Daleo
A practical handbook for parents and teachers wishing to instill spiritual values in their children. Includes activities involving movement, art, storytelling, music and contemplation to explore the core values of balance, mindfulness, self-reliance, compassion and joy.

The Little Goo-Roo: Lessons From Your Baby
By Jan Kirschner and Tracy Kirschner
A warm and delightful book to remind us of life's lessons we never outgrow.

Meditating With Children: The Art of Concentration and Centering
By Deborah Rozman, Ph.D.
Teaches children to center in the heart with guided imagery, yoga postures, creative fantasy, movement, and love.

Moonbeam: A Book of Meditations for Children.
By Maureen Garth
Simple visualizations for parents to help children to awaken their creativity, sleep more peacefully, develop concentration, and quiet fears.

I Saw A Purple Cow and 100 Other Recipes for Learning
By Ann Cole and Carolyn Haas
This book was published 25 years ago and it became an immediate classic in the field of Early Childhood Education. It still is.

For Teenagers!
What Are You Doing With Your Life?
By J. Krishnamurti, Kishore Khairnar, and Dale Carlson
Great wisdom, sharp guidance, right to the point, especially for teenagers.

ABOUT THE AUTHOR

Ivonne Delaflor, author, teacher, and spiritual practitioner is a certified Parent Talk Trainer and Director of The Parent Talk System in Mexico. She is currently studying Child Psychology at the Stratford Career Institute. As a strong supporter of conscious evolution and God's Realization for all children of the world, Ivonne founded the Mastery Life A.C non-profit organization from Mexico in 2002 which offers lectures, workshops and conscious tools for parents to guide children in their full potential as blessed human beings.

Called by her friends a modern female saint for her active work with children and Parents, she is a survivor of a near death experience at the age of 18 that turned her life into a spiritual quest. She began to meet with recognized spiritual teachers worldwide and today shares her passion through offering free workshops and intuitive wisdom in respecting and allowing children to be who they really are.

She is the creator of the twelve-module workshop *Rediscovering Yourself Through Your Personal Power*. She is also the author of the book and Audio Cd of *The Soulmate Called God, Books I and II, La Maestria de La Vida* published in Mexico by Alom Editores (www.hipnosis.com.mx), and *India, The Journey of a Lifetime*. She is currently working on a workbook entitled *Practical Exercises for the Positive Child,* the profits of which will go to the orphanage LA CASITA DE CANCUN. She is also co-authoring a book for children that will be donated to the Waldorf School of Santa Barbara, California.

She conducts regular free workshops in Cancun, Mexico and through her Mastery Life Organization assists spiritual teachers such as Doreen Virtue, Chick Moorman, Alan Cohen and many others to share their wisdom in raising the consciousness and awareness that it is through love that children will evolve and teach us their peaceful ways.

A percentage of the profits of this book, *The Positive Child* will be donated to the creation of a conscious community in Mexico that will benefit the Mayan and orphan children of Cancun.

Ivonne currently lives with her husband and her two children in California. You may contact her through her website: http://www.masterylife.com/ or you can send email at idelaflor@masterylife.com

0-595-66469-5

Printed in the United States
23924LVS00001B/133-141